A Complete Assembly of all Maps & Plans from
SIR CHARLES OMAN'S ATLAS
OF THE PENINSULAR WAR

The Naval & Military Press Ltd

Published by

The Naval & Military Press Ltd
Unit 5 Riverside, Brambleside
Bellbrook Industrial Estate
Uckfield, East Sussex
TN22 1QQ England

Tel: +44 (0)1825 749494

www.naval-military-press.com
www.nmarchive.com

*In reprinting in facsimile from the original, any imperfections are inevitably reproduced
and the quality may fall short of modern type and cartographic standards.*

Index to maps

Maps from Volume 1

1. Saragossa.
2. Battle of Medina de Rio Seco. July 14, 1808.
3. Battle of Baylen. July 19, 1818 at the moment of Dupont's third attack. Part of Andalusia, between Andujar and the Passes. July 19, 1808.
4. Battle of Vimiero. August 21, 1808.
5. Catalonia.
6. Part of Northern Spain.
7. Battle of Espinosa. November 11, 1818.
   Madrid in 1808.
   Battle of Tudela. November 23, 1808.
8. Battle of Corunna. January 16, 1809.
9. Large Map of Spain and Portugal, showing physical features and roads.

Maps from Volume 2

10. Battle of Uclés. January 13, 1809.
    Siege of Rosas. November 6 to December 5, 1809.
11. Part of Catalonia, to illustrate St. Cyr's Campaign. November 1808 to March 1809.
    Battle of Valls. February 25, 1809.
12. Second Siege of Saragossa. December 1808 to February 1809.
13. Battle of Medellin. March 28, 1809.
14. Combat of Braga (Lanhozo). March 20, 1809.
    Oporto. March – May 1809, showing the Portuguese lines.
15. Northern Portugal, to illustrate Marshal Soult's Campaign of March to May 1809.
16. Battle of Alcañiz. May 23, 1809.
    Battle of Maria. June 15, 1809.
17. Battle of Talavera. The Main Engagement. 3 to 5pm, July 28, 1809.
18. Central Spain, showing the localities of the Talavera Campaign. July to August 1809.

Maps from Volume 3

19. Siege of Gerona
20. Battle of Tamames. October 18, 1809.
21. Battle of Ocaña. November 19, 1809.
22. Andalusia, to illustrate the Campaign of 1810.
23. Topography of Cadiz and its environs.
24. Central Portugal.
25. Siege of Astorga.
26. Siege of Ciudad Rodrigo.
27. Combat of the Coa. July 24, 1810.
28. General Map of Catalonia.
29. The Mondego Valley.
30. Battle of Bussaco. September 27, 1810.
31. Ney's attack at Bussaco.
32. Reynier's attack at Bussaco.
33. The Lines of Torres Vedras.

Maps from Volume 4

34. Badajoz (the French Siege, January to March 1811), and the Battle of the Gebora (February 19, 1811).
35. The Battle of Barrosa.
36. General Map of the Barrosa Campaign.
37. Combat of Redinha
38. Combat of Casal Novo
39. Combat of Foz d'Arouce
40. The Lower Mondego. To illustrate the first Siege of Massena's Retreat. Leiria to the Alva River
41. Combat of Sabugal
42. Map to illustrate the last stage of Massena's Retreat and the Campaign of Fuentes de Oñoro.
43. Plan of the Siege of Tortosa
44. The two British Sieges of Badajoz in May and June 1811.
45. Battle of Fuentes de Oñoro. Positions on the first day, May 3, 1811.
46. Battle of Fuentes de Oñoro. May 5, 1811.
47. Battle of Albuera No. 1. (About 10am)
48. Battle of Albuera No. 2. (About 11.30am)
49. General Map of Estremadura.
50. Plan of the Siege of Tarragona.
51. General Map of Catalonia.

Maps from Volume 5

52. General Theatre of the Suchet's Campaigns in Eastern Spain. Valencia, 1811–1812.
53. Plan of the Battle of Saguntum.
54. Suchet's Valencia. The Siege. December 1811 to January 1812.
55. General Map of Catalonia.
56. Plan of Tarifa.
57. Plan of the Siege Operations at Ciudad Rodrigo.
58. Plan of the Siege Operations at Badajoz.
59. Map of the District Round Almaraz.
60. General Map of Central Spain, to illustrate the Salamanca Campaign.
61. Plan of the Salamanca Forts.
62. The Salamanca Campaign. Map of the country between Salamanca and Tordesillas.
63. General Plan of the Battle of Salamanca.
64. The Last Episode at Salamanca. Part of the field showing approximate position at the moment of advance of the 6th Division about 7pm. Combat of Garcia Hernandez. July 23, 1812.
65. General Map of Estremadura to illustrate Hill's Campaigns in March-April and June-August 1812.

Maps from Volume 6

66. Plan of the Siege Operations at Burgos. September – October 1812.
67. Operations around Salamanca/Almeida region illustrating the Salamanca retreat of November 1812.
68. Battle of Castalla. April 13, 1813.
69. The Campaign of Vittoria. May 22 to June 21, 1813.
70. Plan of the Battle of Vittoria.
71. Attack of St. Sebastian between July 11 and September 9, 1813.
72. General Map of the country between Bayonne and Pamplona.
73. Combat of Roncesvalles. July 25, 1813.
74. Combat of Maya. July 25, 1813.
75. First Battle of Sorauren. July 28, 1813 showing the general situation at 1.15pm.
76. Second Battle of Sorauren and Combat of Beunza. July 30, 1813.

Maps from Volume 7

77. Battle of San Marcial. August 31, 1813.
78. Catalonia. Inset: the country between Barcelona and Tarragona showing the localities of Bentinck's Bampaign of 1813.
79. Passage of the Bidasso. October 7, 1813.
80. Storm of the French lines above Vera. October 17, 1813.
81. Battle of the Nivelle. November 10, 1813.
82. Battle of the Nive. December 10, 1813.
83. Battle of St. Pierre at the moment of Hill's Counterstroke. December 13, 1813.
84. The country and the roads between Bayonne and Orthez to illustrate the Campaign of February 1814.
85. Battle of Orthez. February 27, 1814.
86. Combat of Aire. March 2, 1814.
87. Operations round Bordeaux. March – April 1814.
88. Orthez to Toulouse. February 27 – April 11, 1814.
89. Combat of Tarbes. March 20, 1814.
90. The Toulouse Country. March 26 – April 14, 1814.
91. Battle of Toulouse. April 10, 1814.

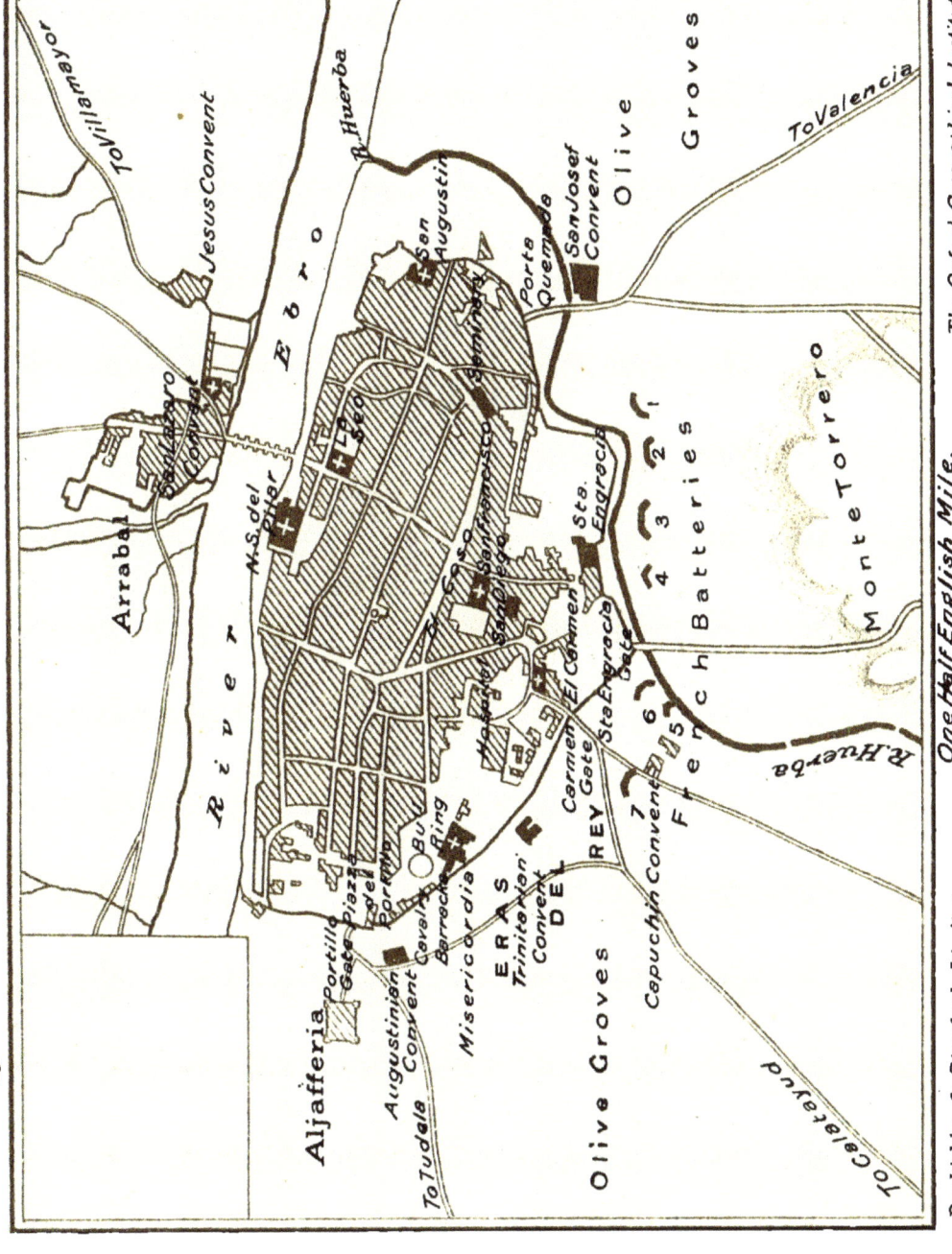

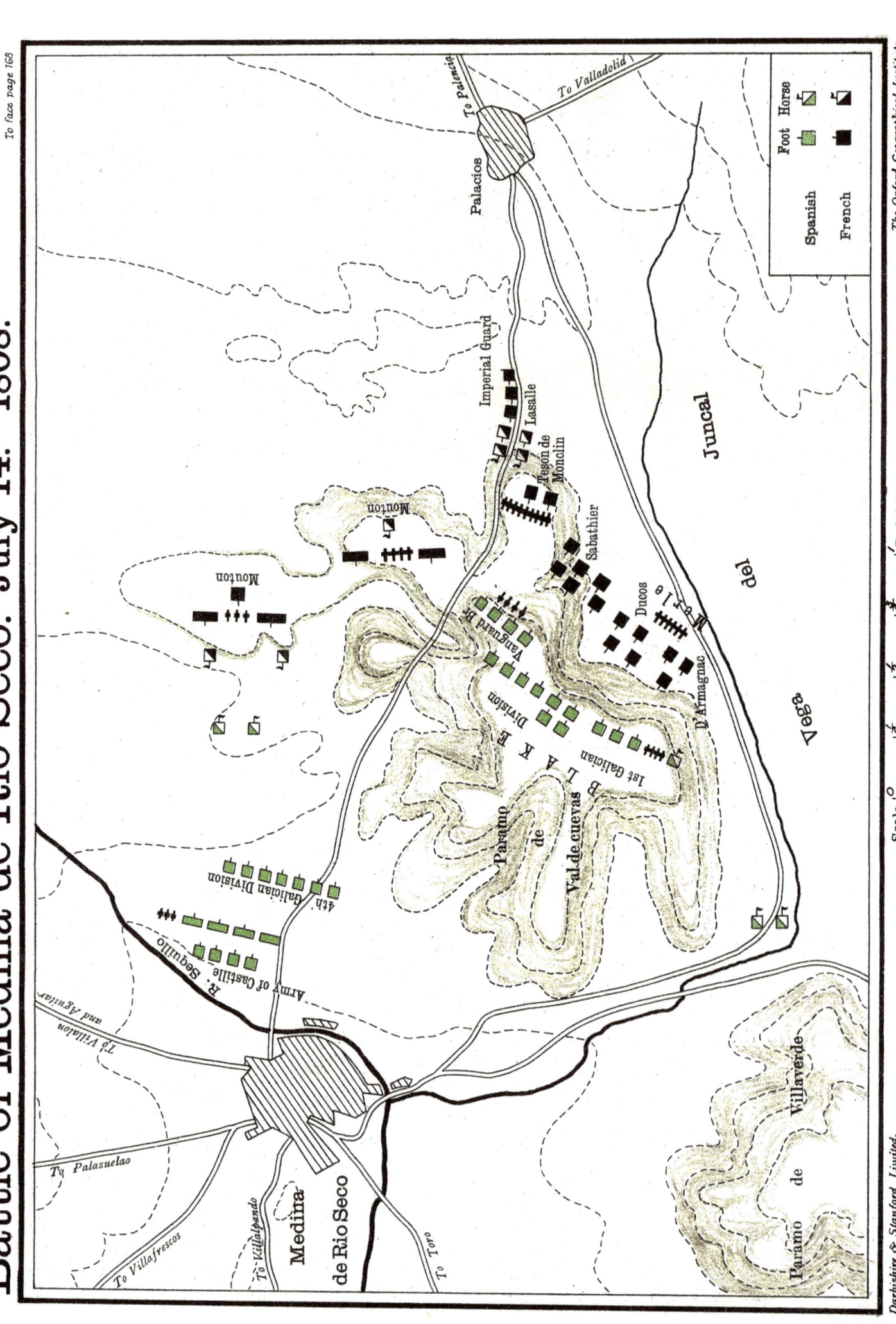

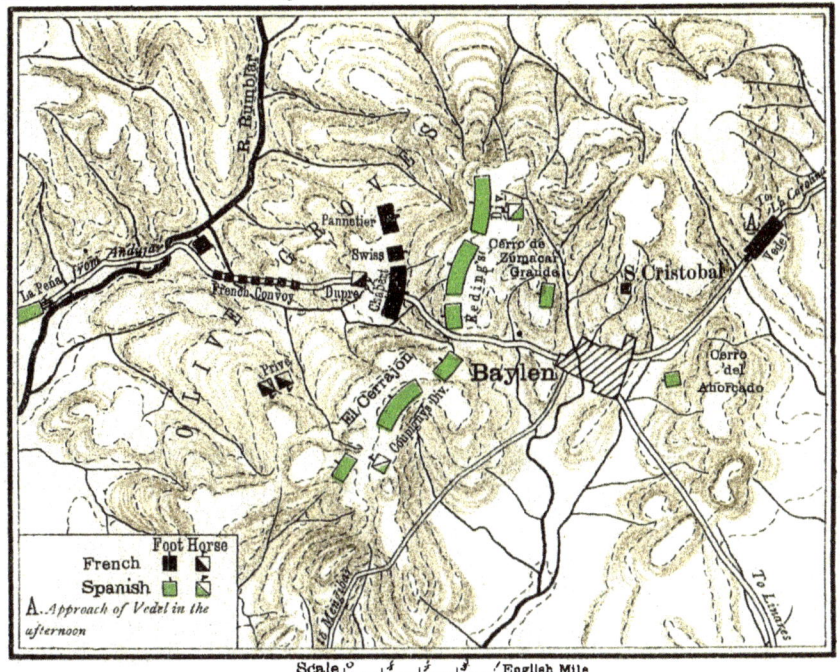

Battle of BAYLEN July 19, 1808, at the moment of DUPONT'S third attack.

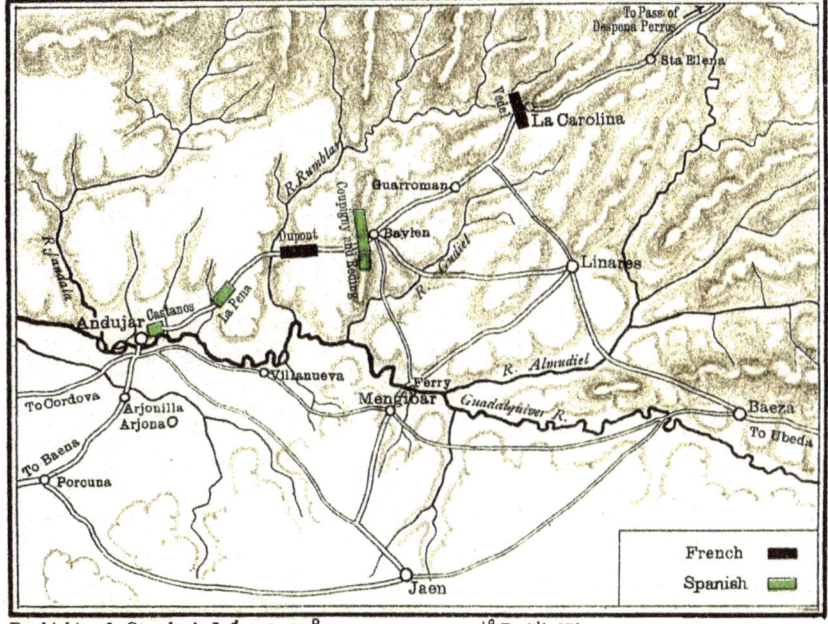

Part of ANDALUSIA, between Andujar and the Passes. July 19, 1808.

Battle of Vimiero. August 21. 1808.

Catalonia.

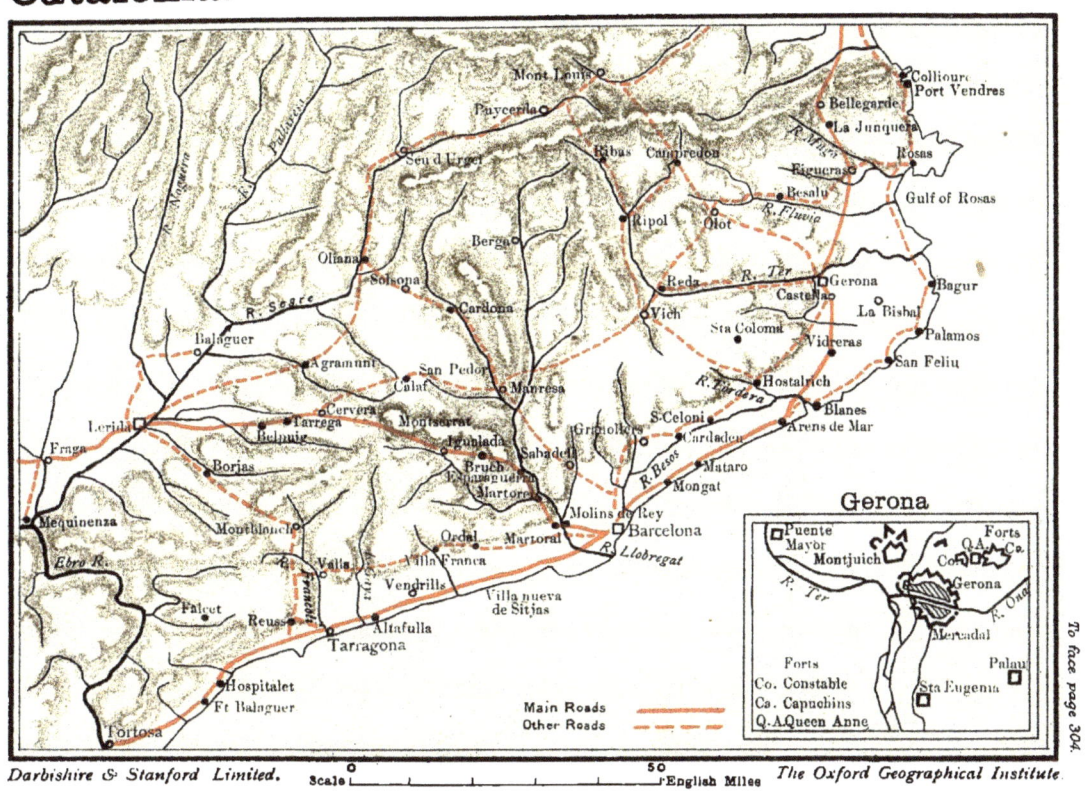

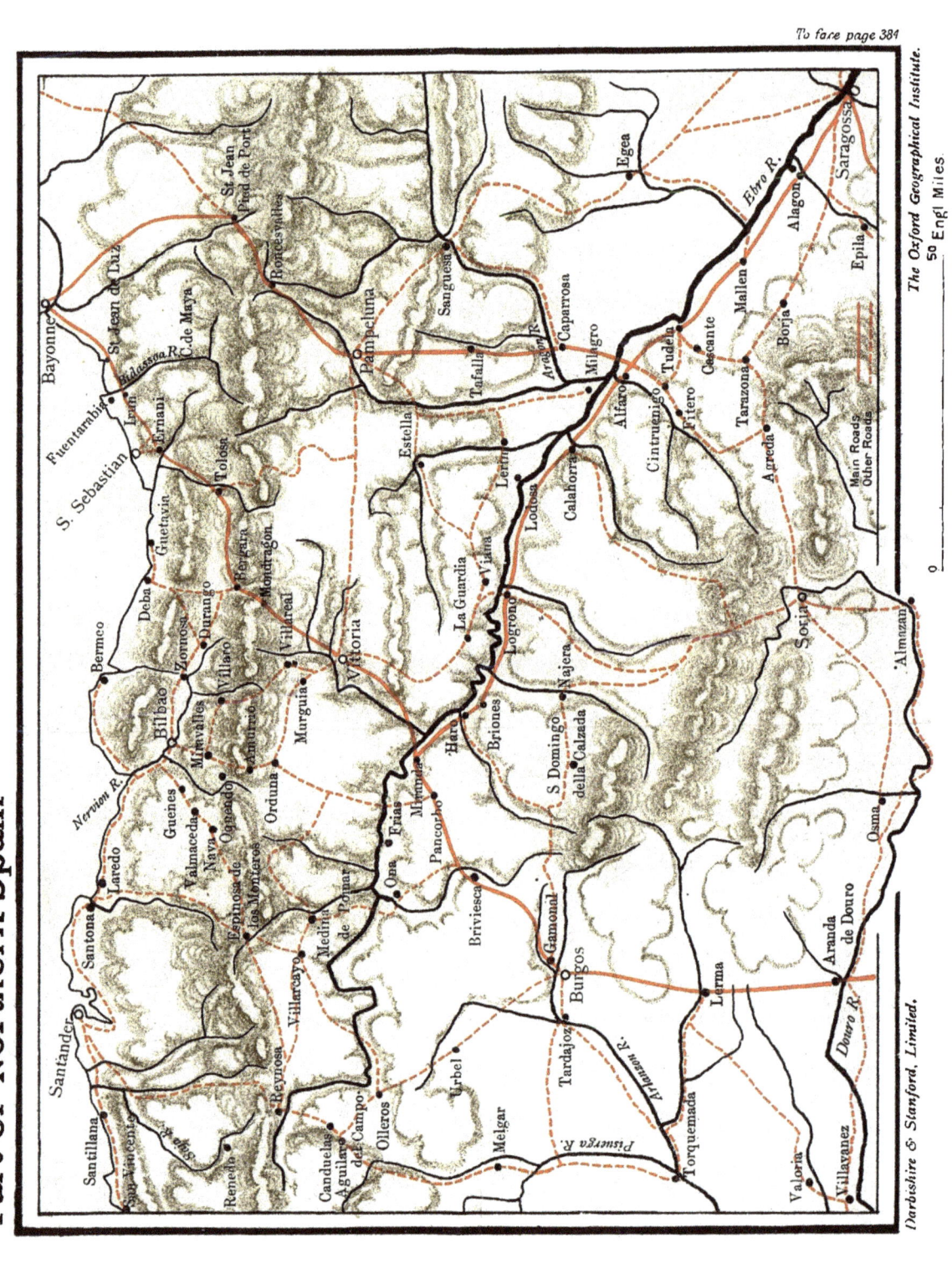

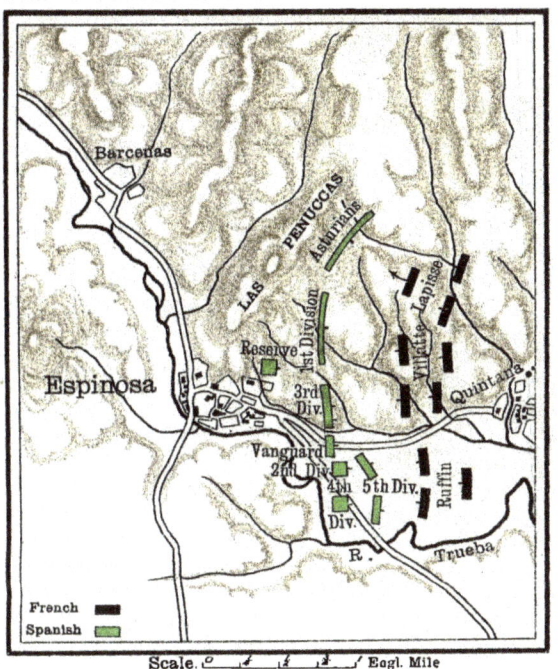

Battle of ESPINOSA. November 11th. 1808

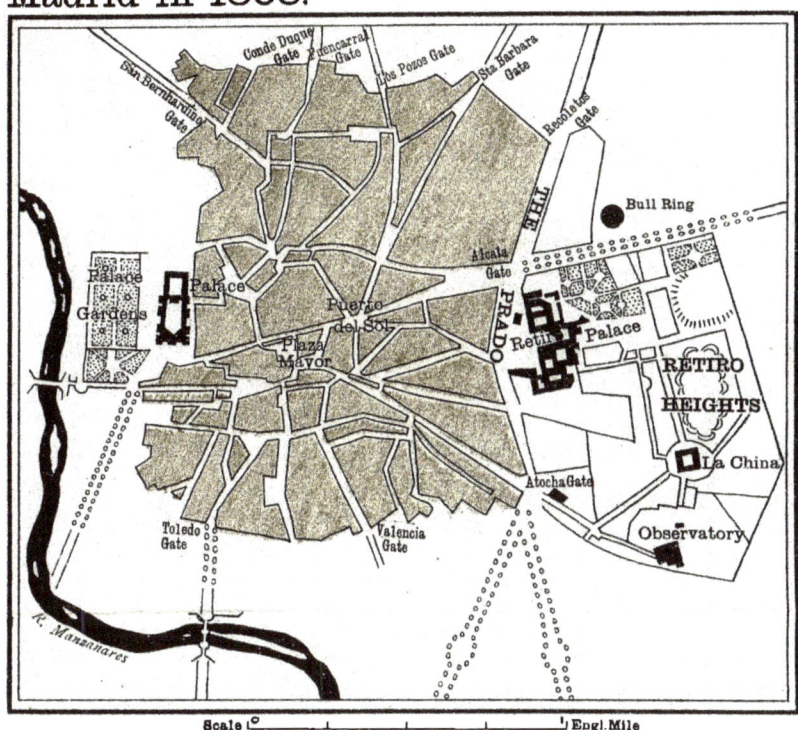

Madrid in 1808.

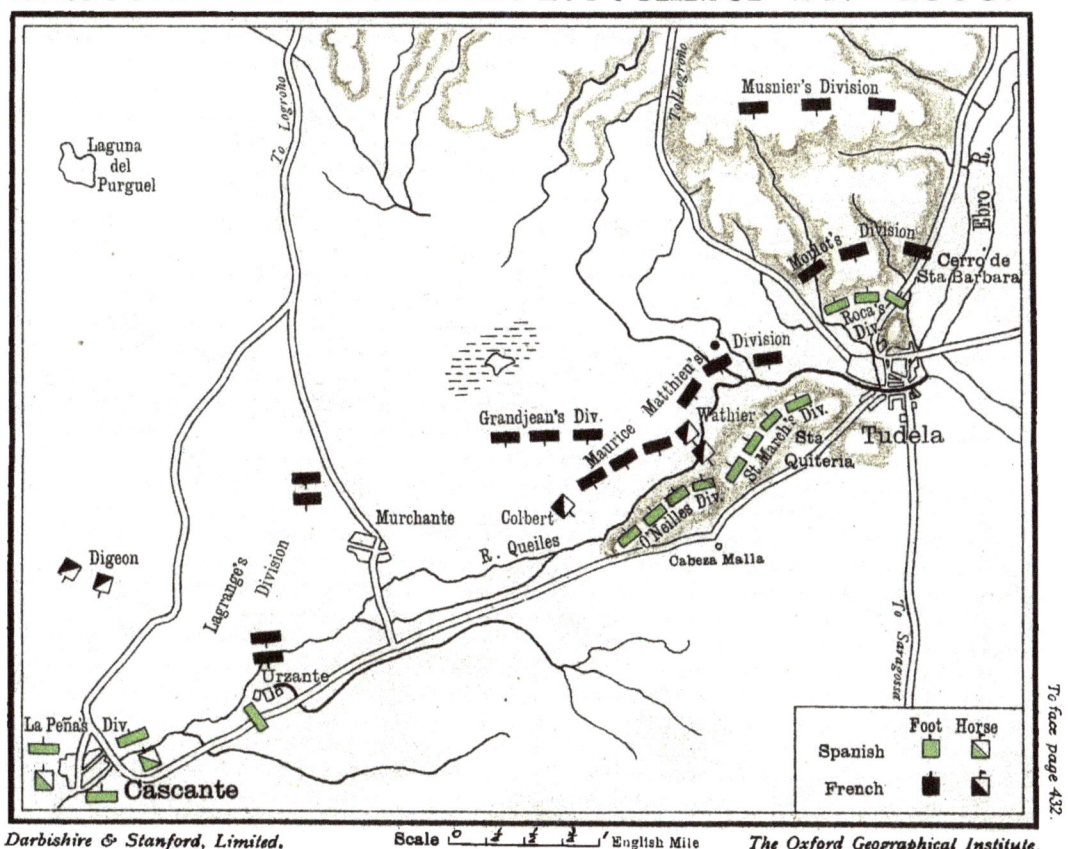

Battle of Tudela. November 23. 1808.

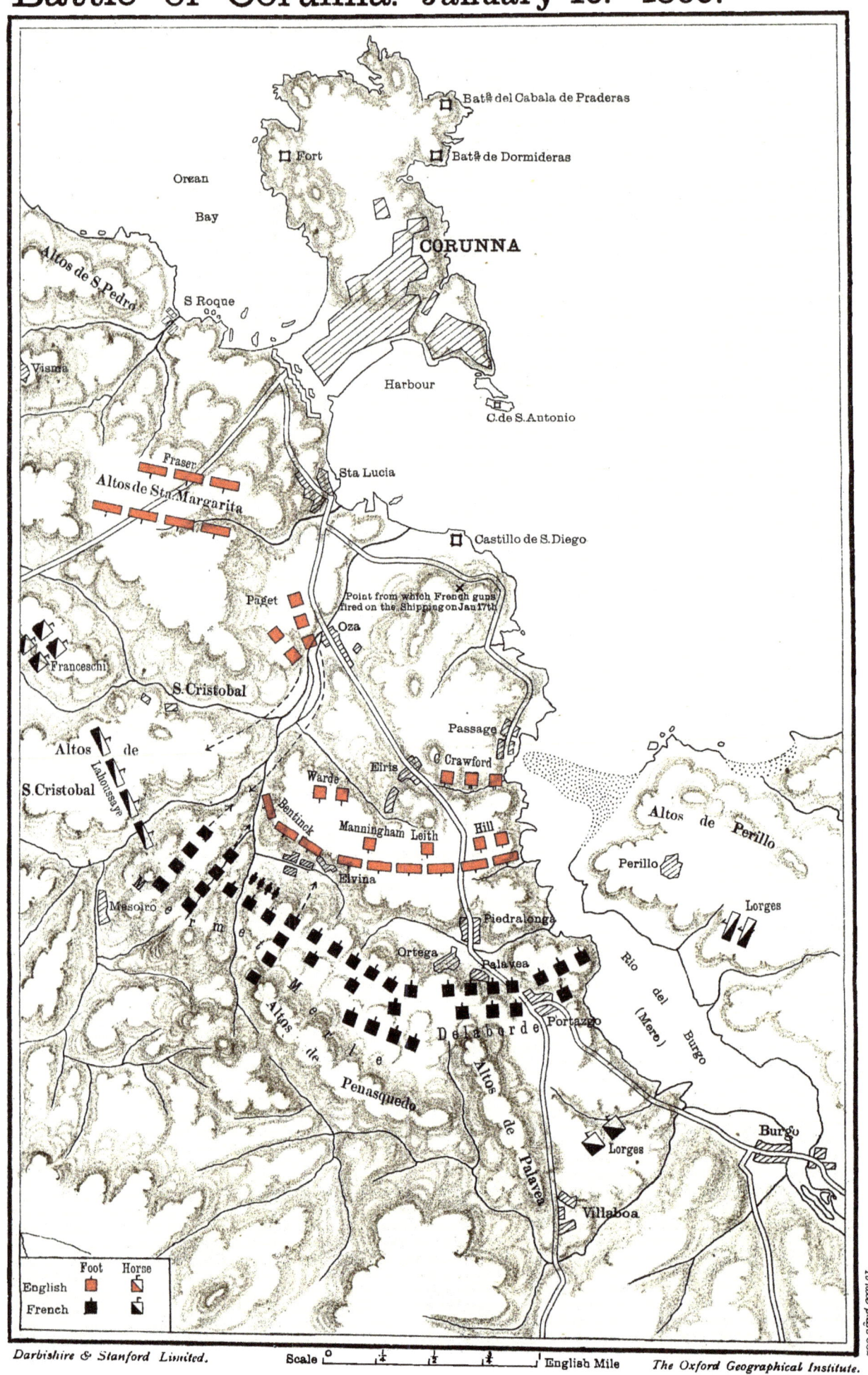

Spain and Portugal, showing physical features and roads.

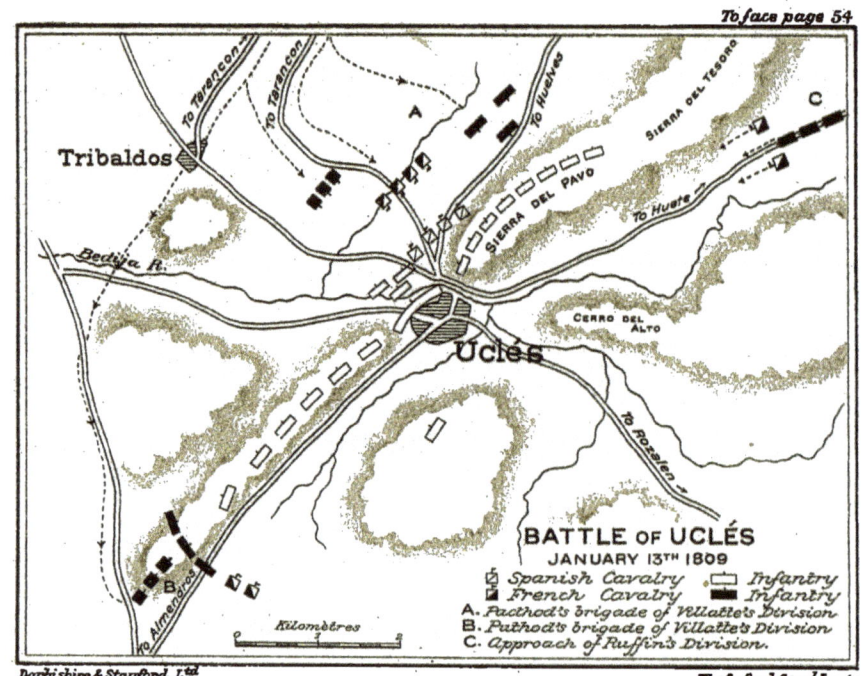

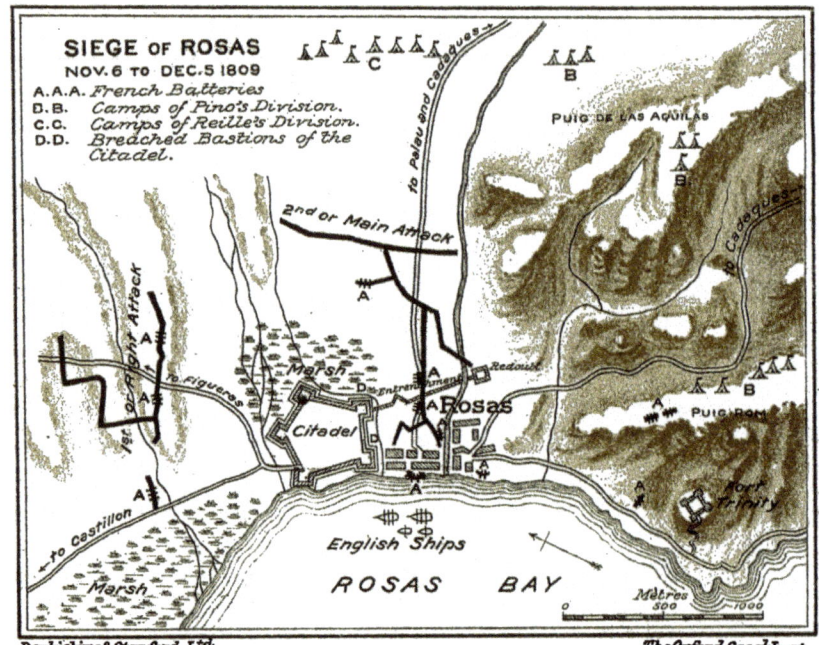

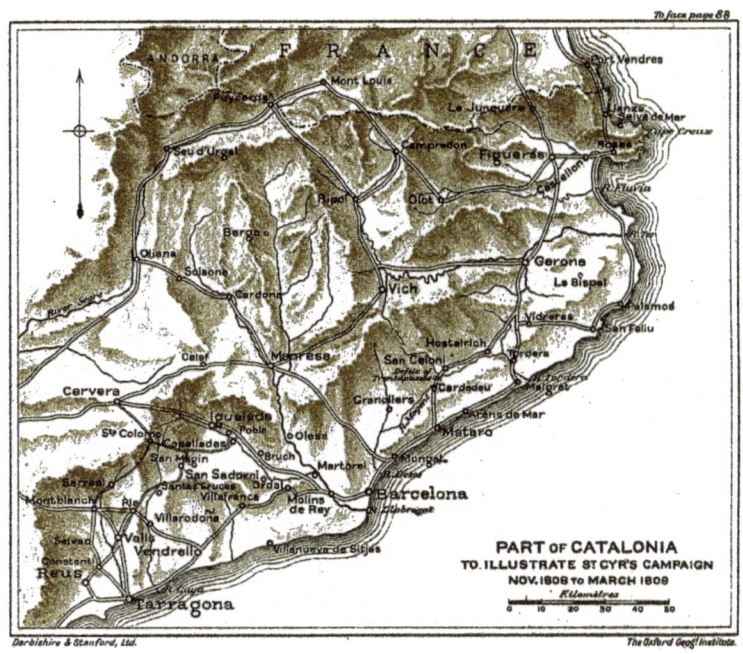

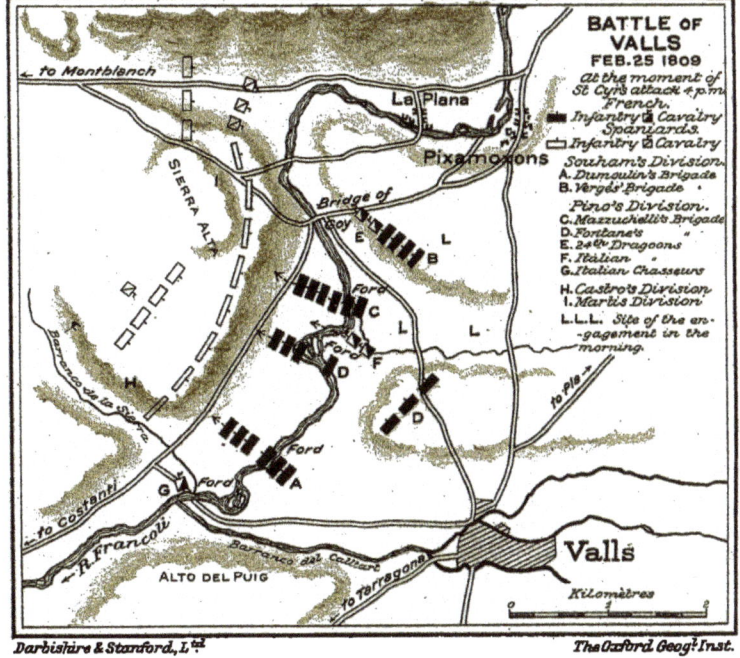

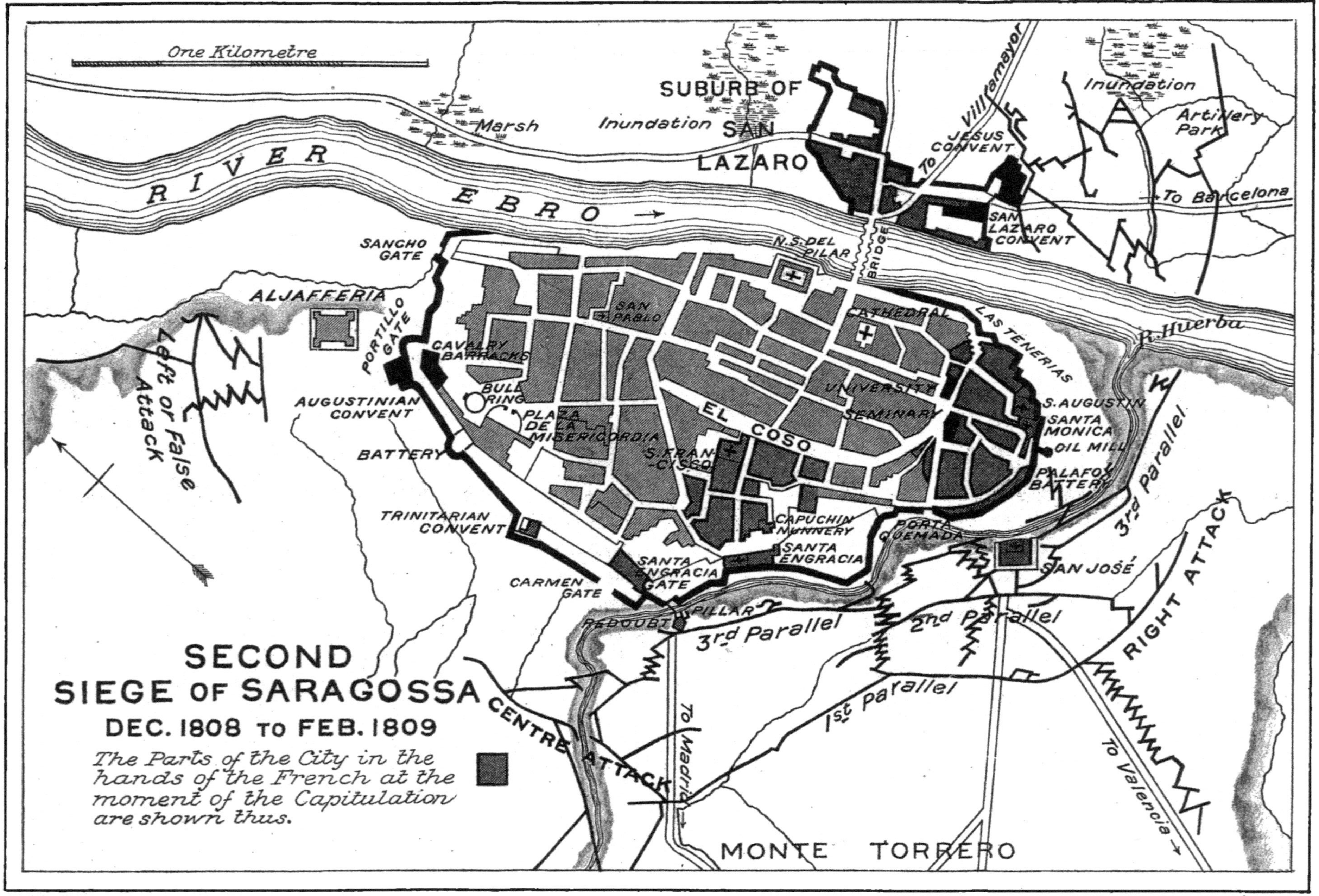

Darbishire & Stanford Ltd. The Oxford Geog! Institute

BATTLE of MEDELLIN
MARCH 28TH 1809

French,
■ Infantry ◧ Cavalry
Spaniards.
☐ Infantry ◱ Cavalry

A.A. Extreme points reached by advance of Spanish left wing.
B.B. Extreme points reached by advance of Spanish right wing.

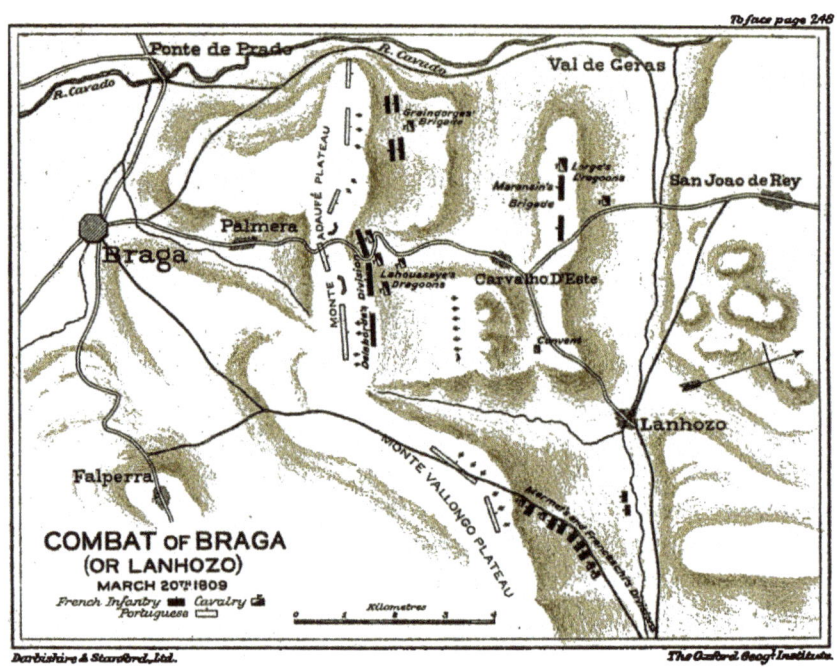

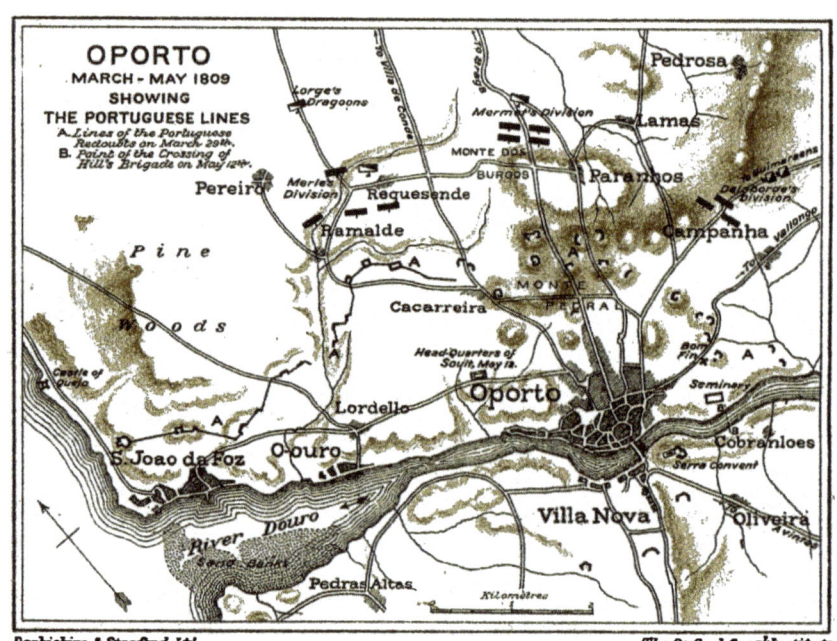

NORTHERN PORTUGAL TO ILLUSTRATE MARSHAL SOULT'S CAMPAIGN OF MARCH TO MAY 1809

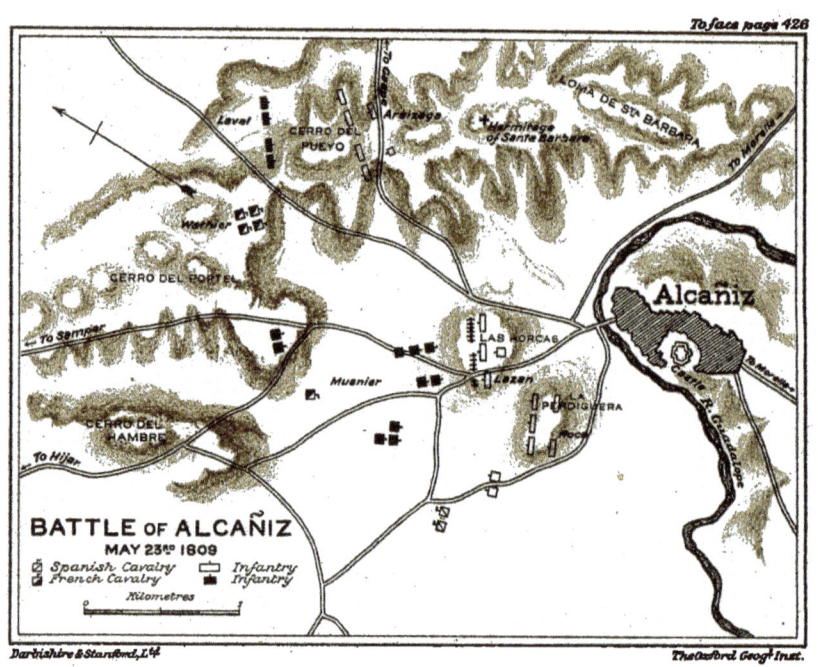

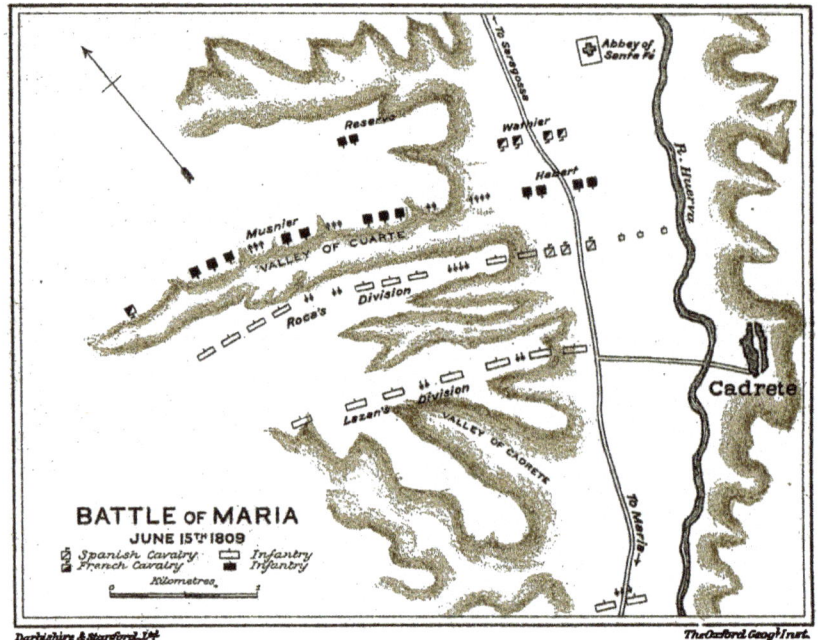

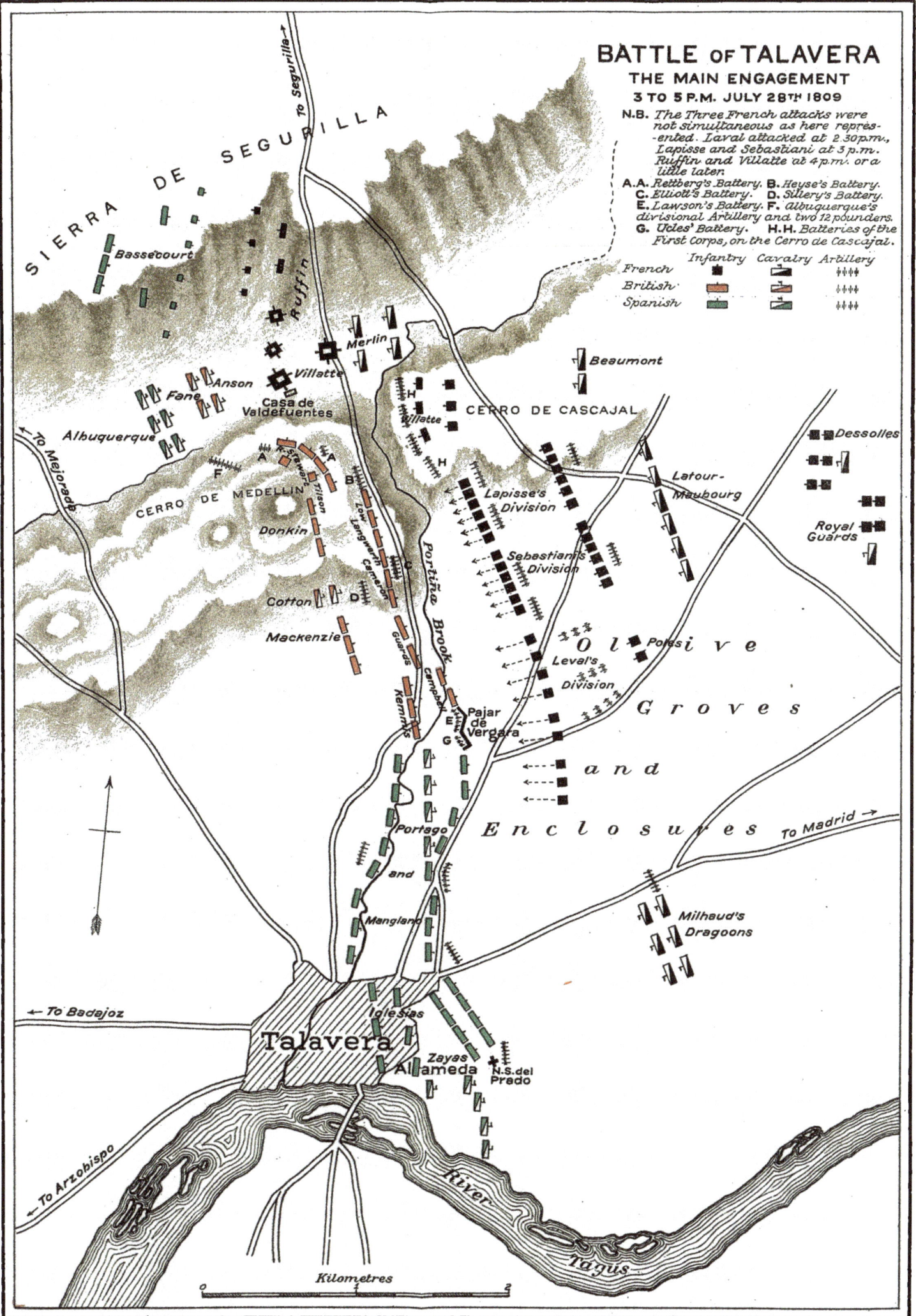

THE CAMPAIGN OF TALAVERA
JULY–AUGUST 1809

ENVIRONS OF ARZOBISPO

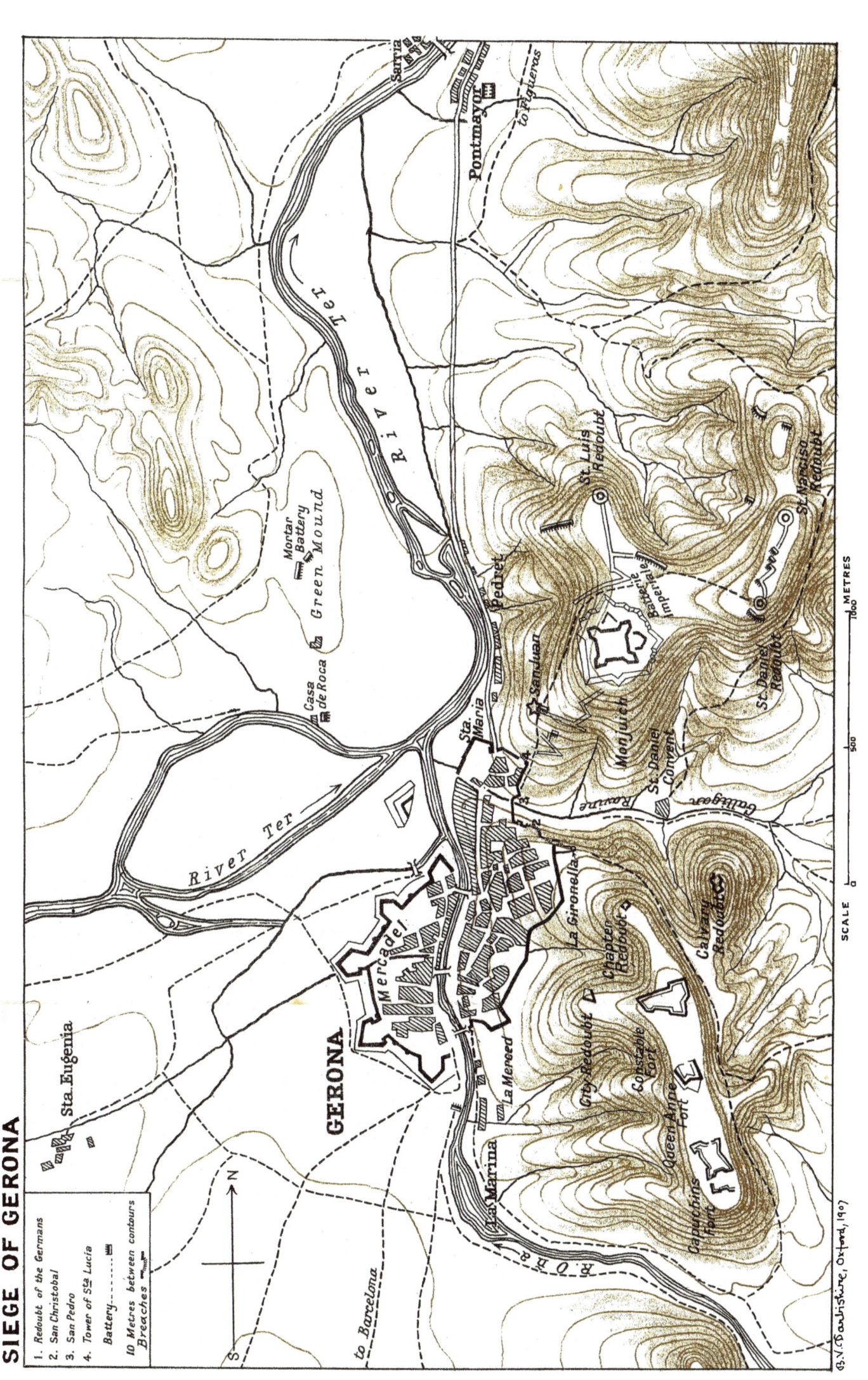

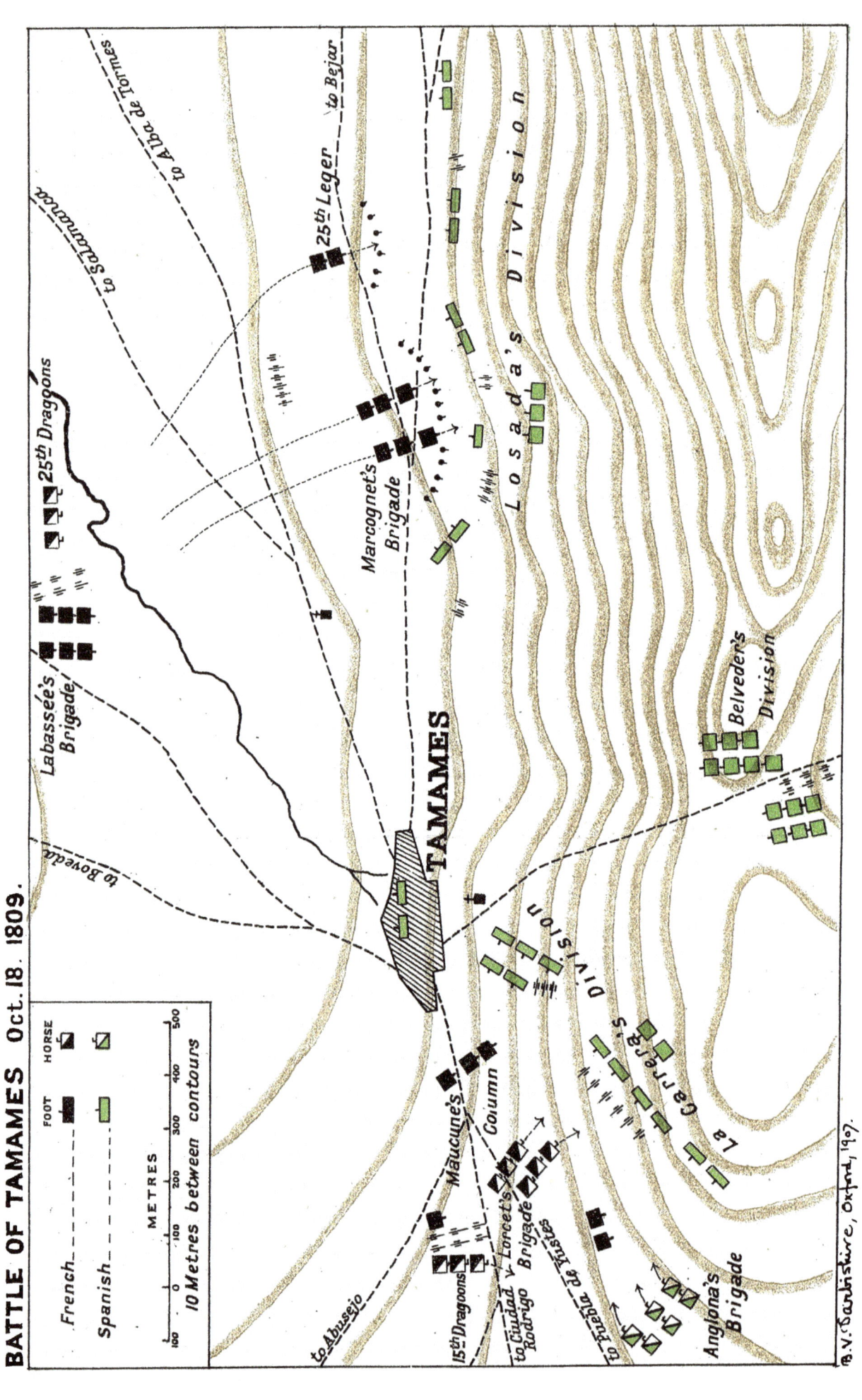

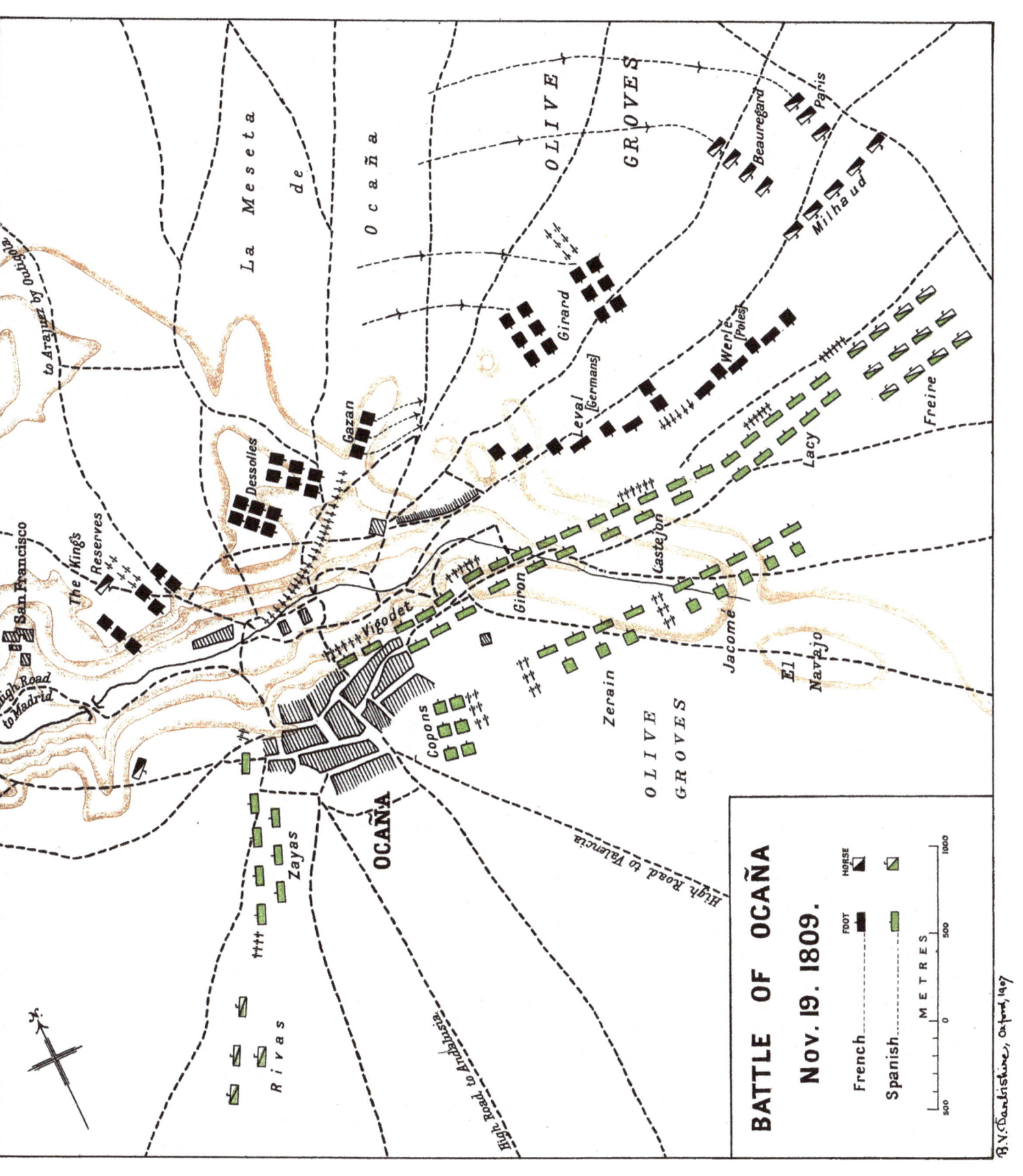

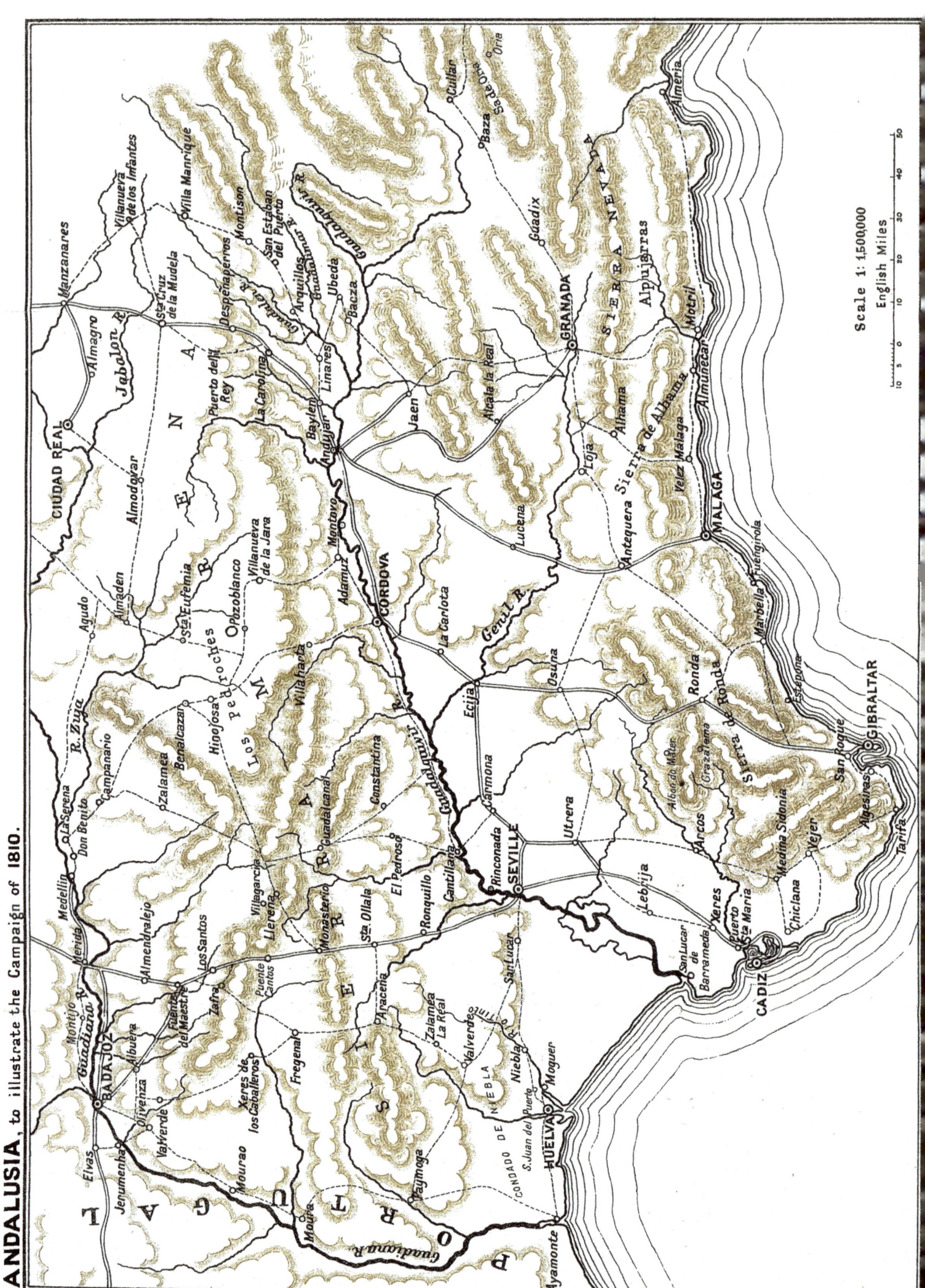

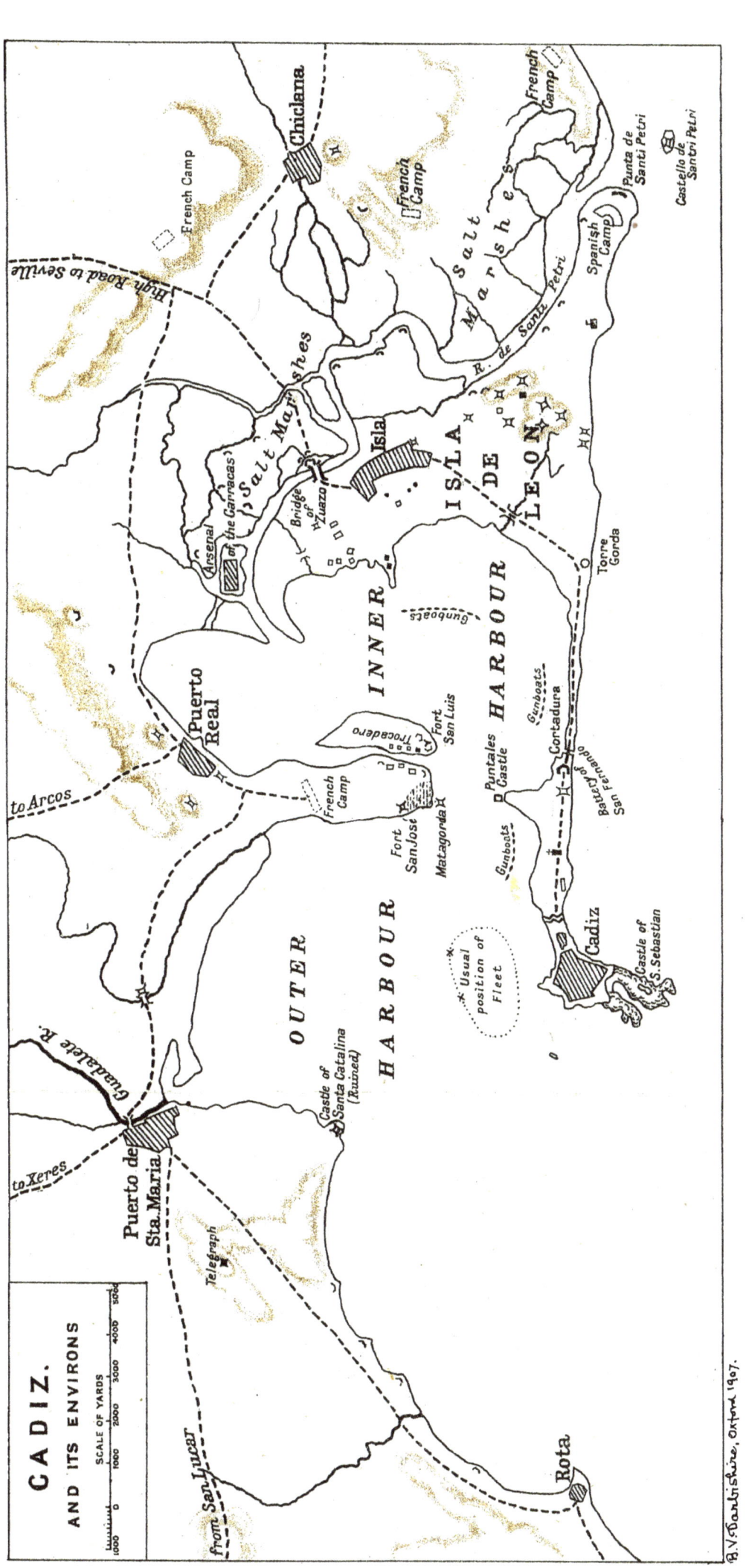

CENTRAL PORTUGAL

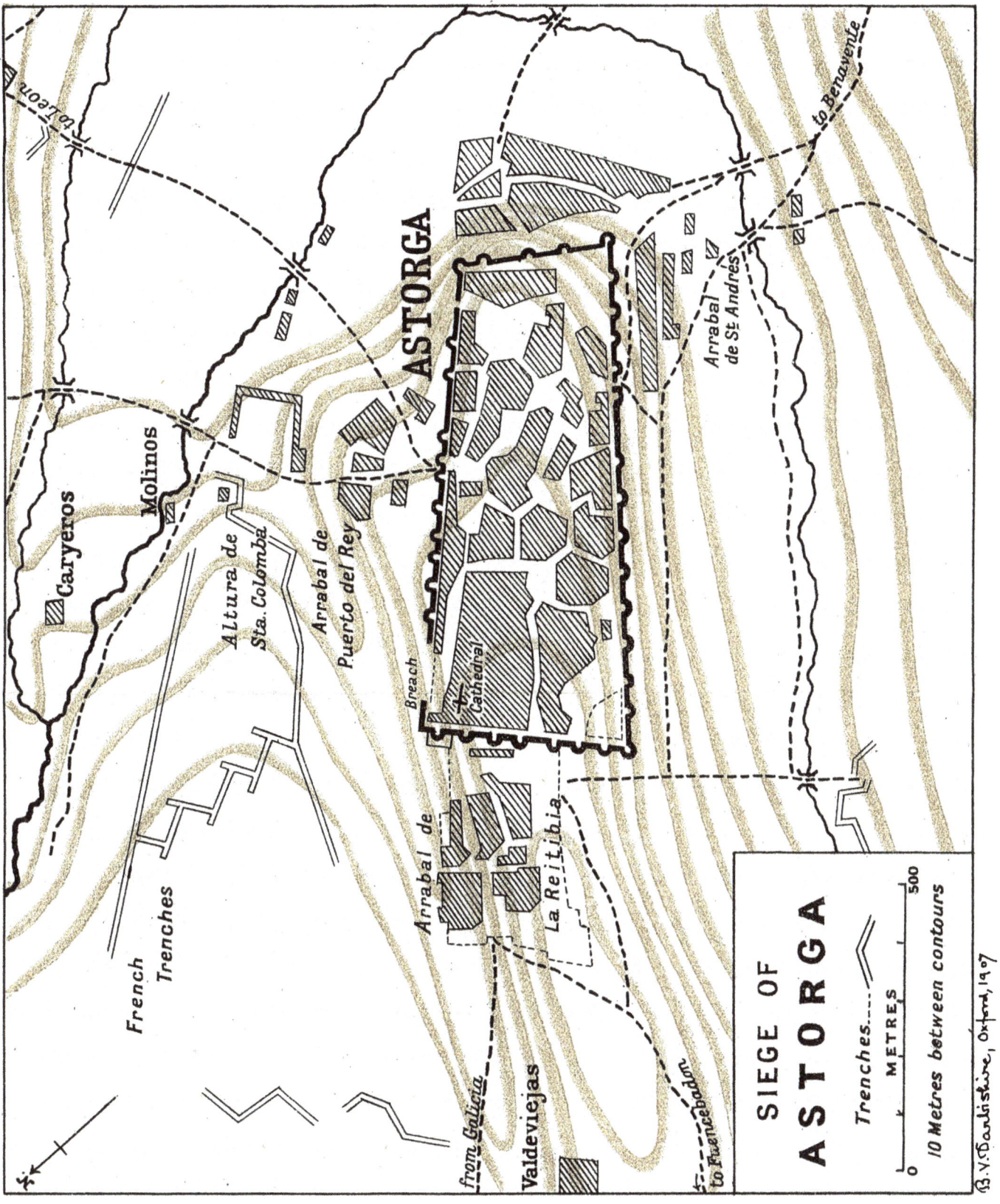

SIEGE OF CIUDAD RODRIGO

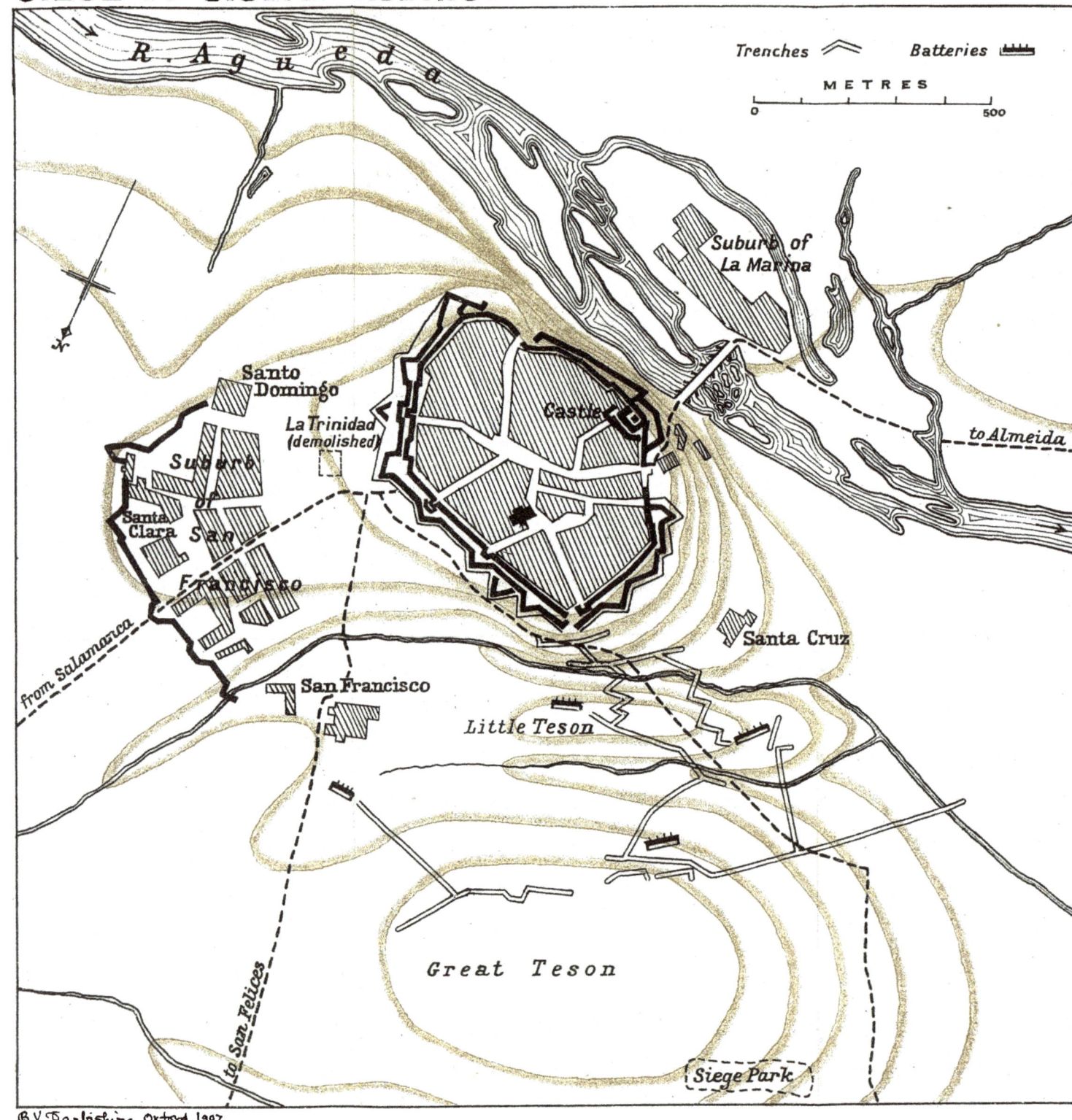

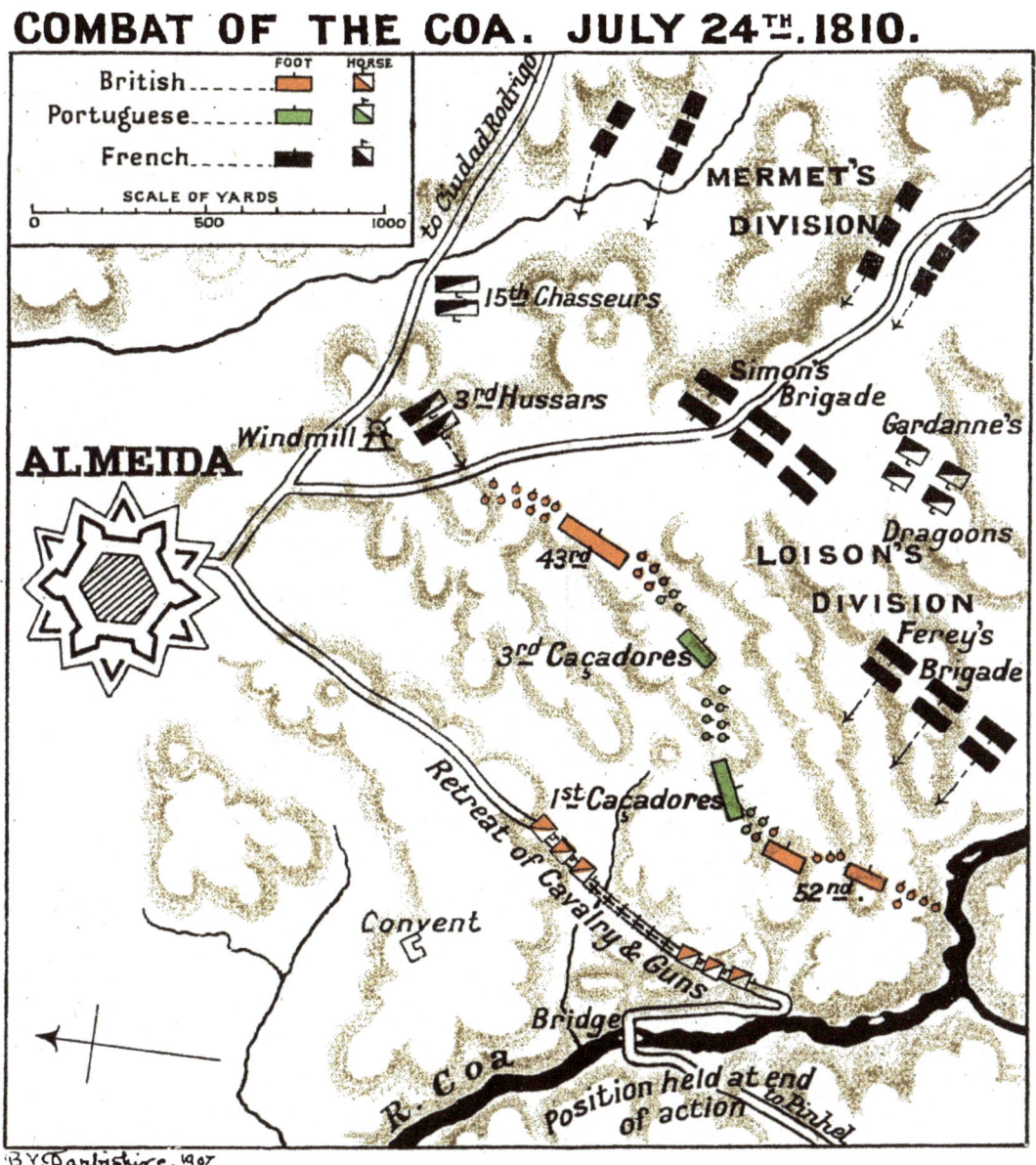

CATALONIA

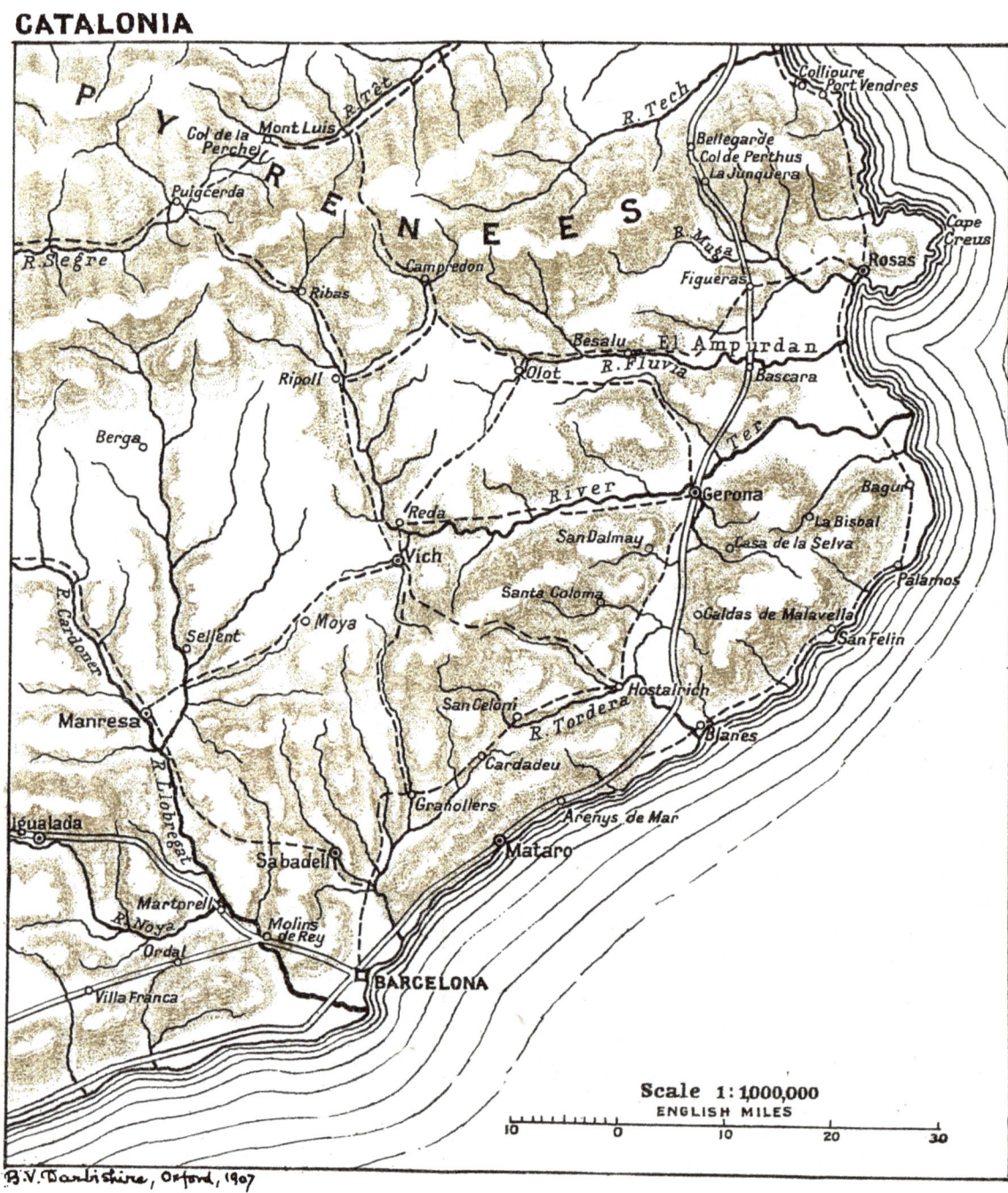

THE MONDEGO VALLEY

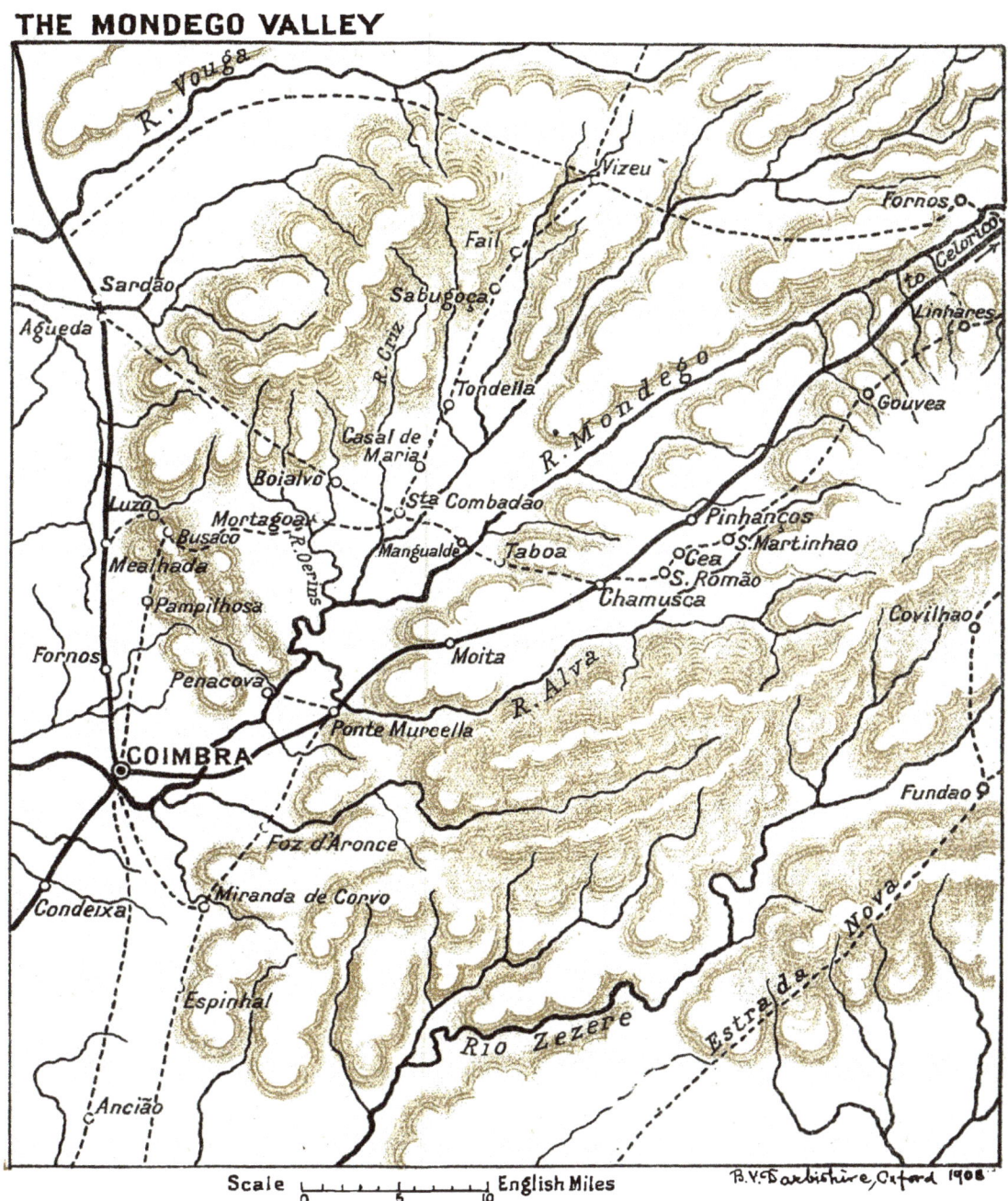

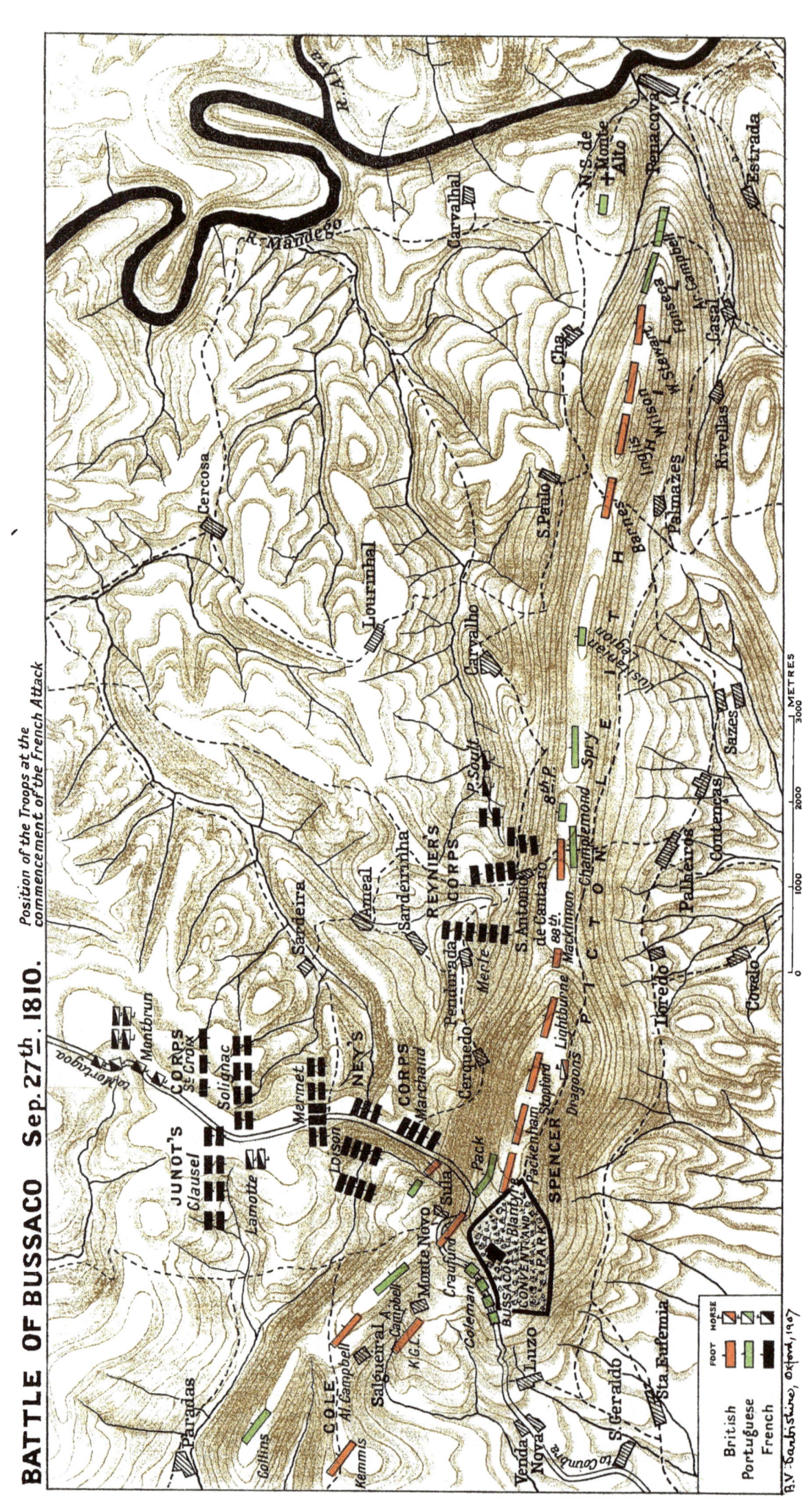

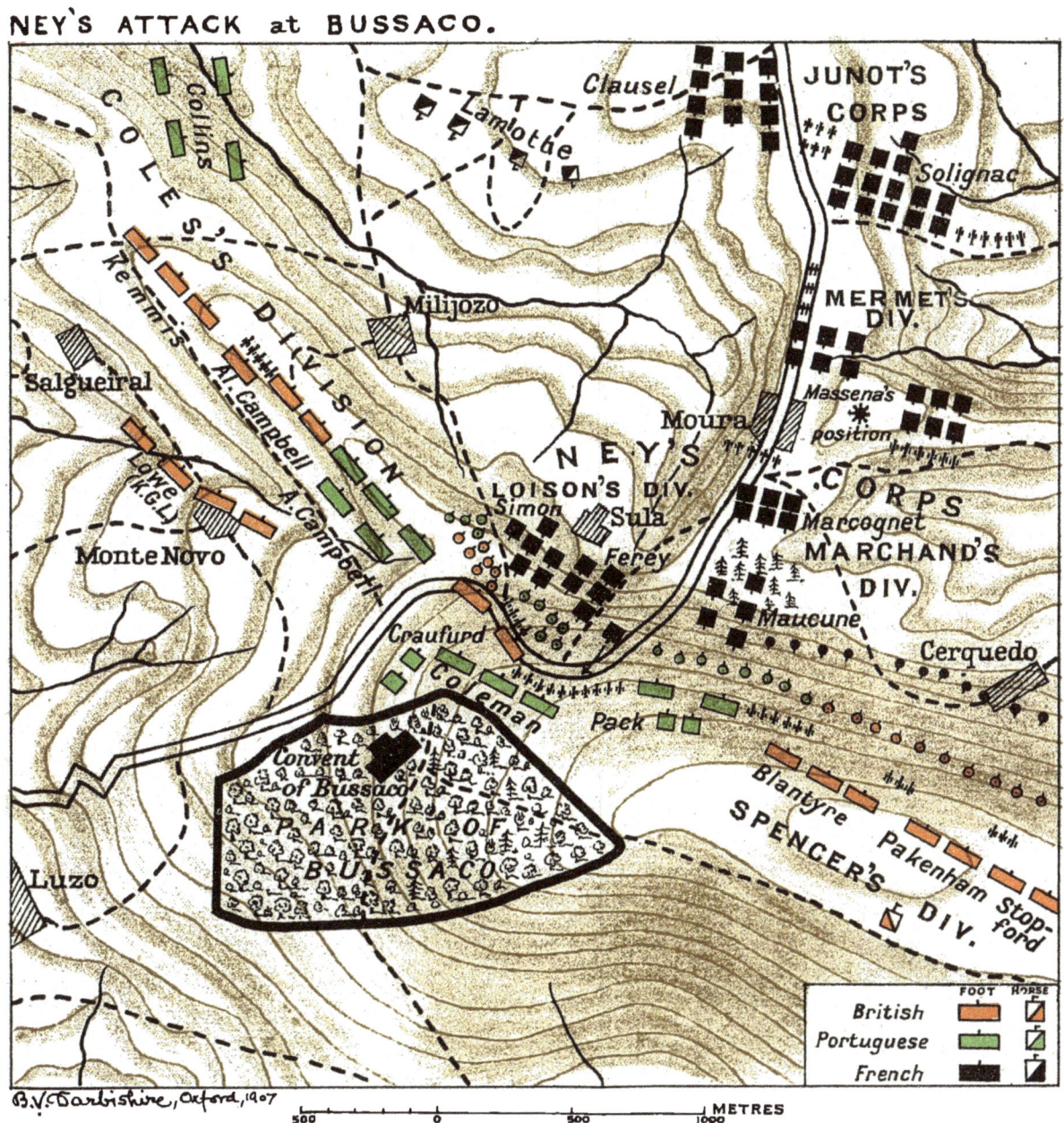

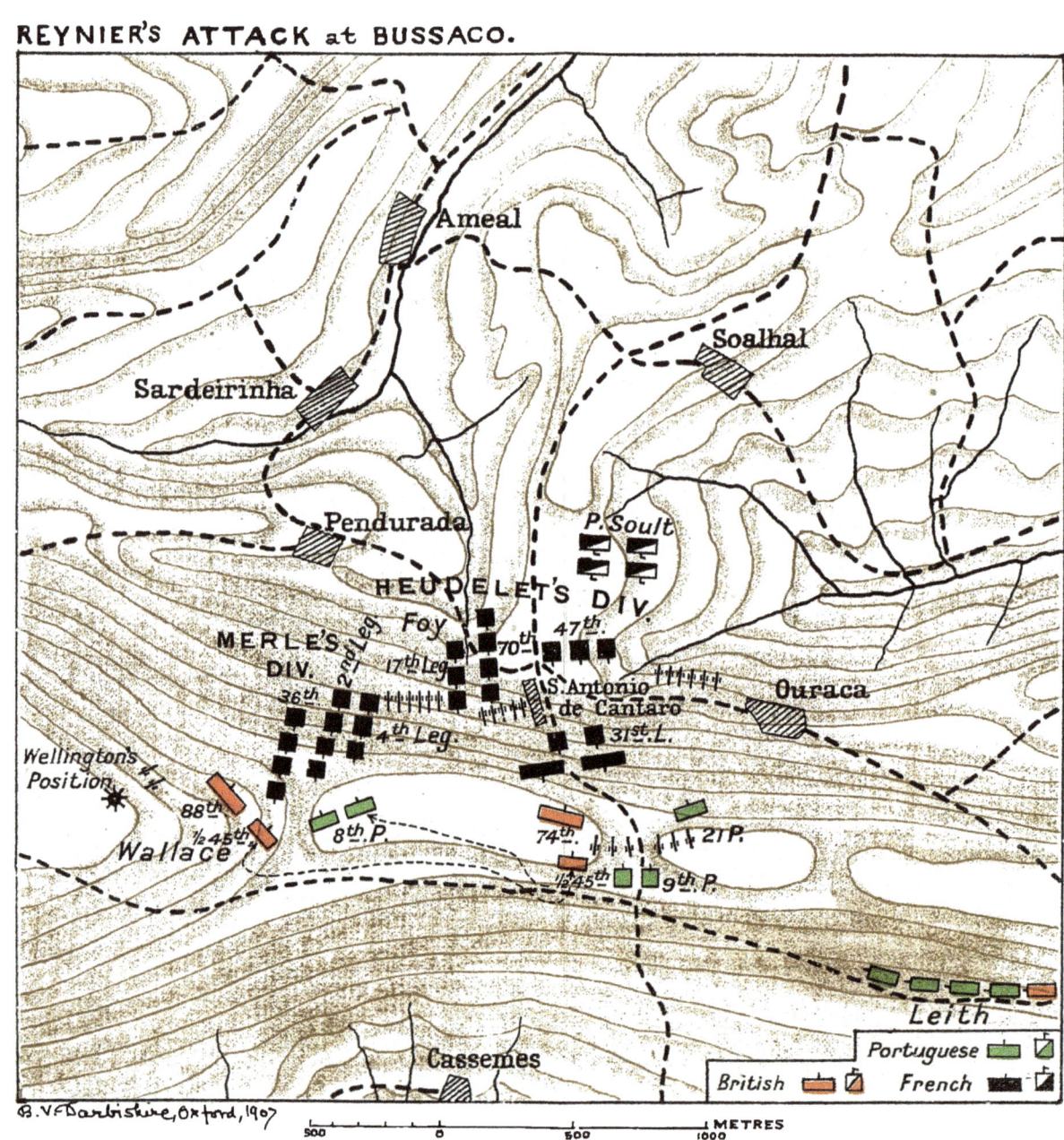

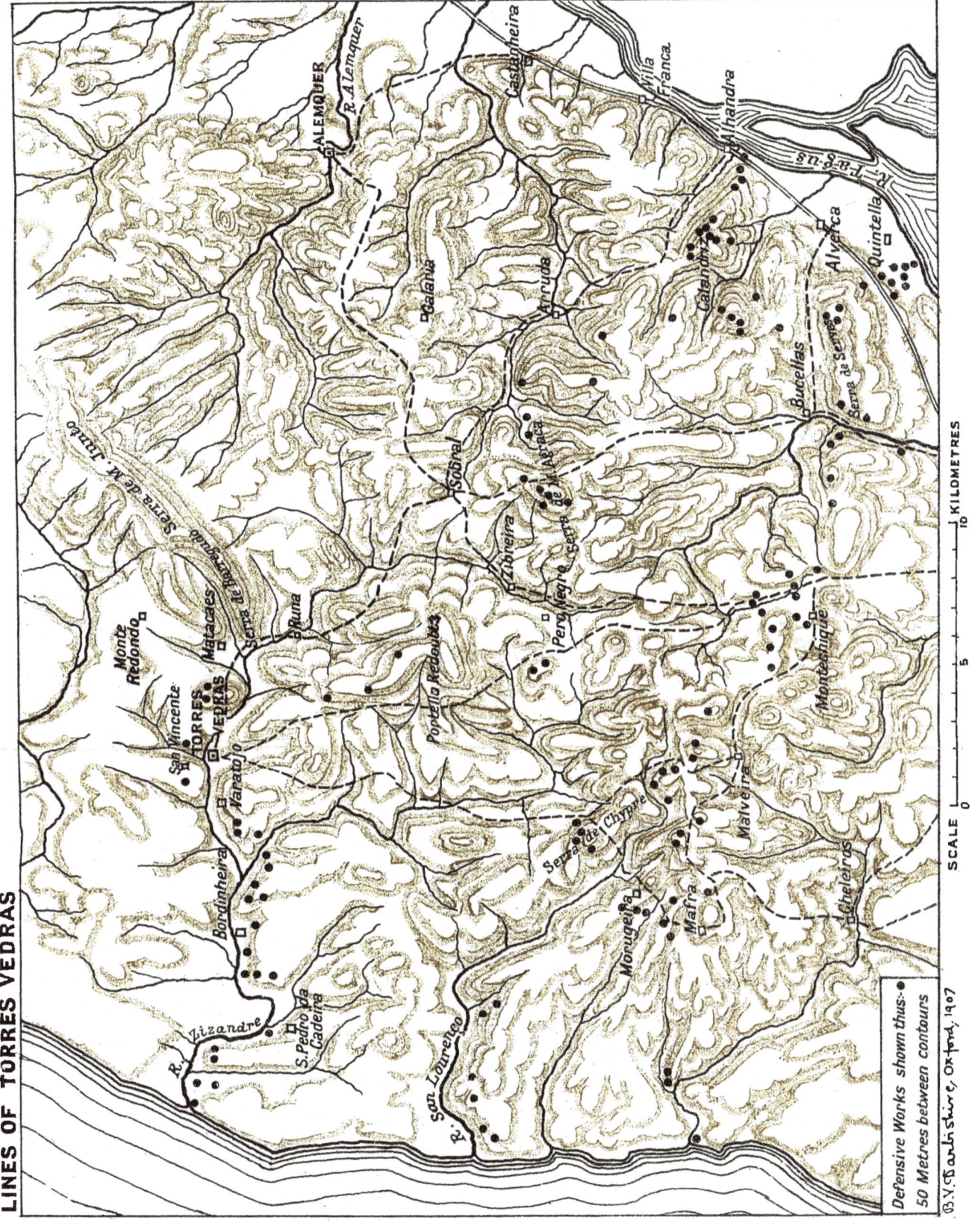

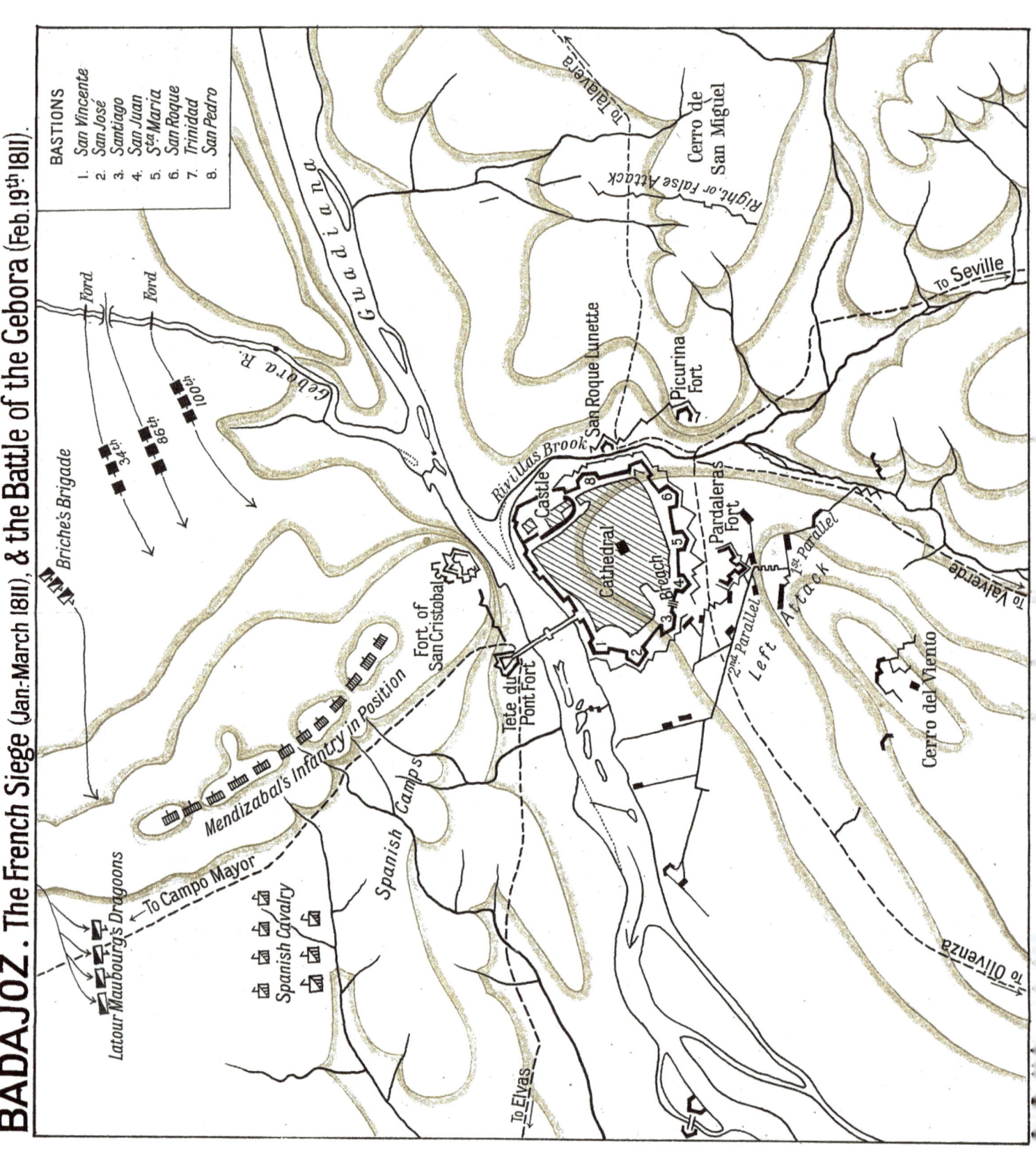

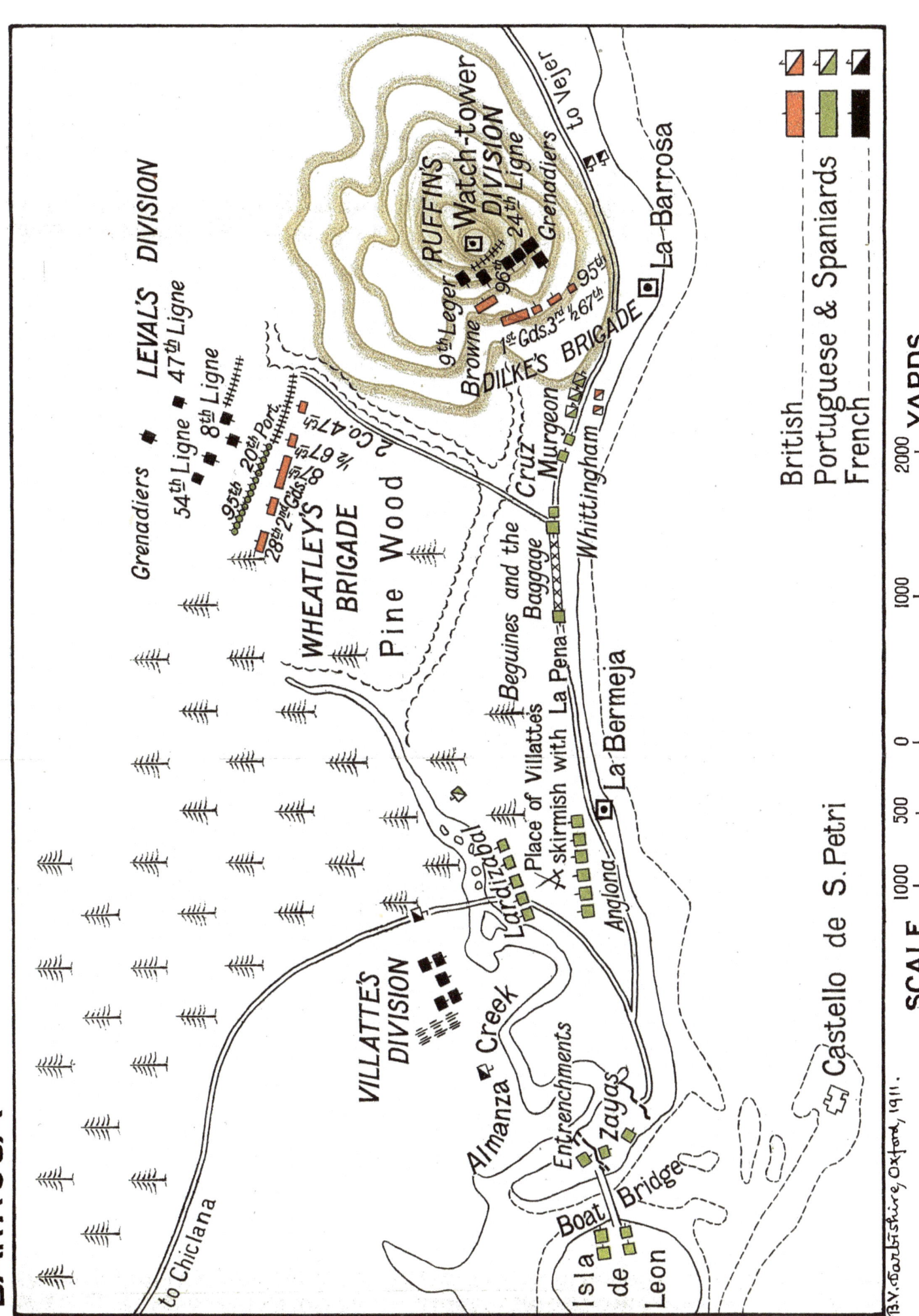

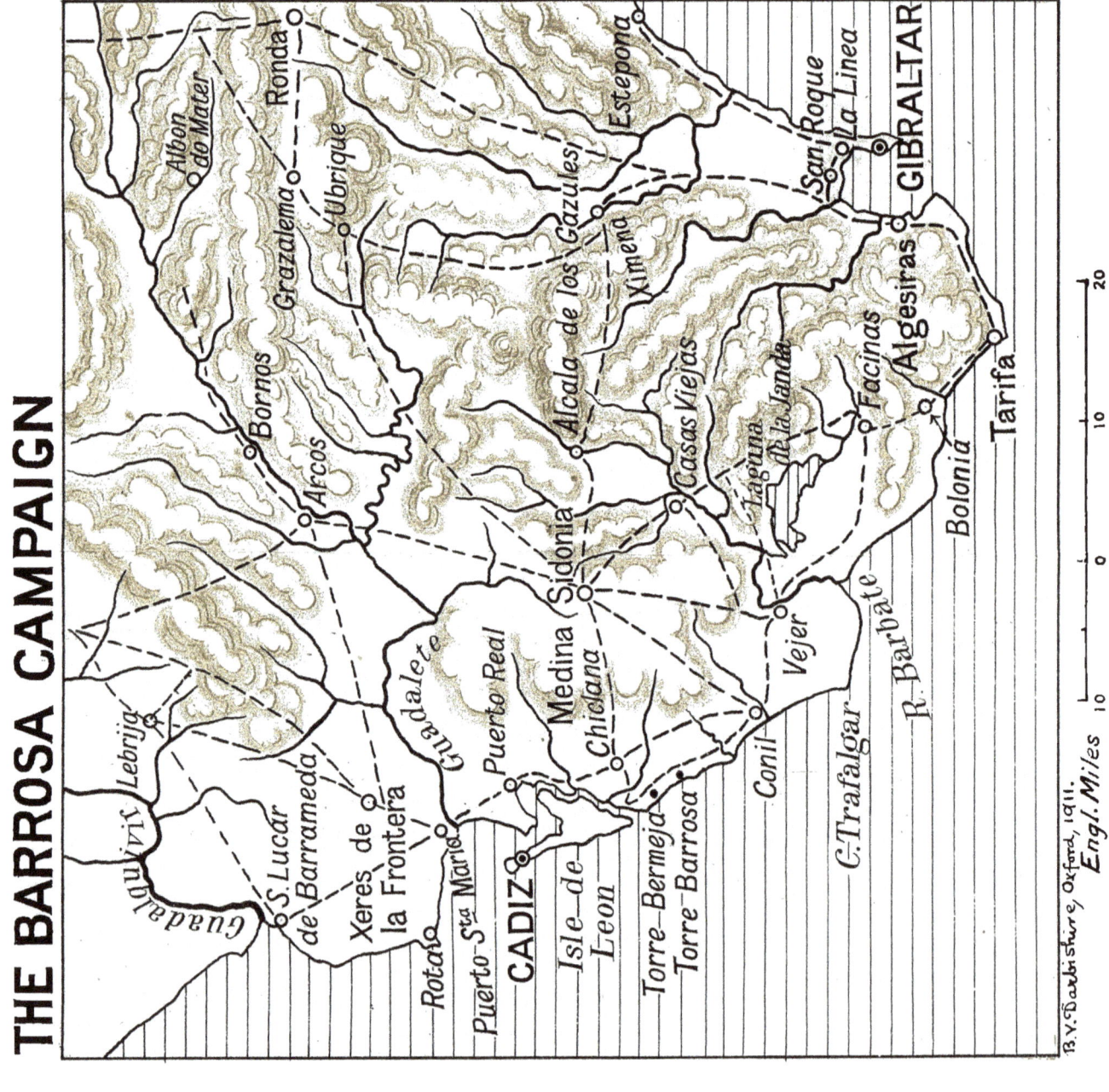
THE BARROSA CAMPAIGN

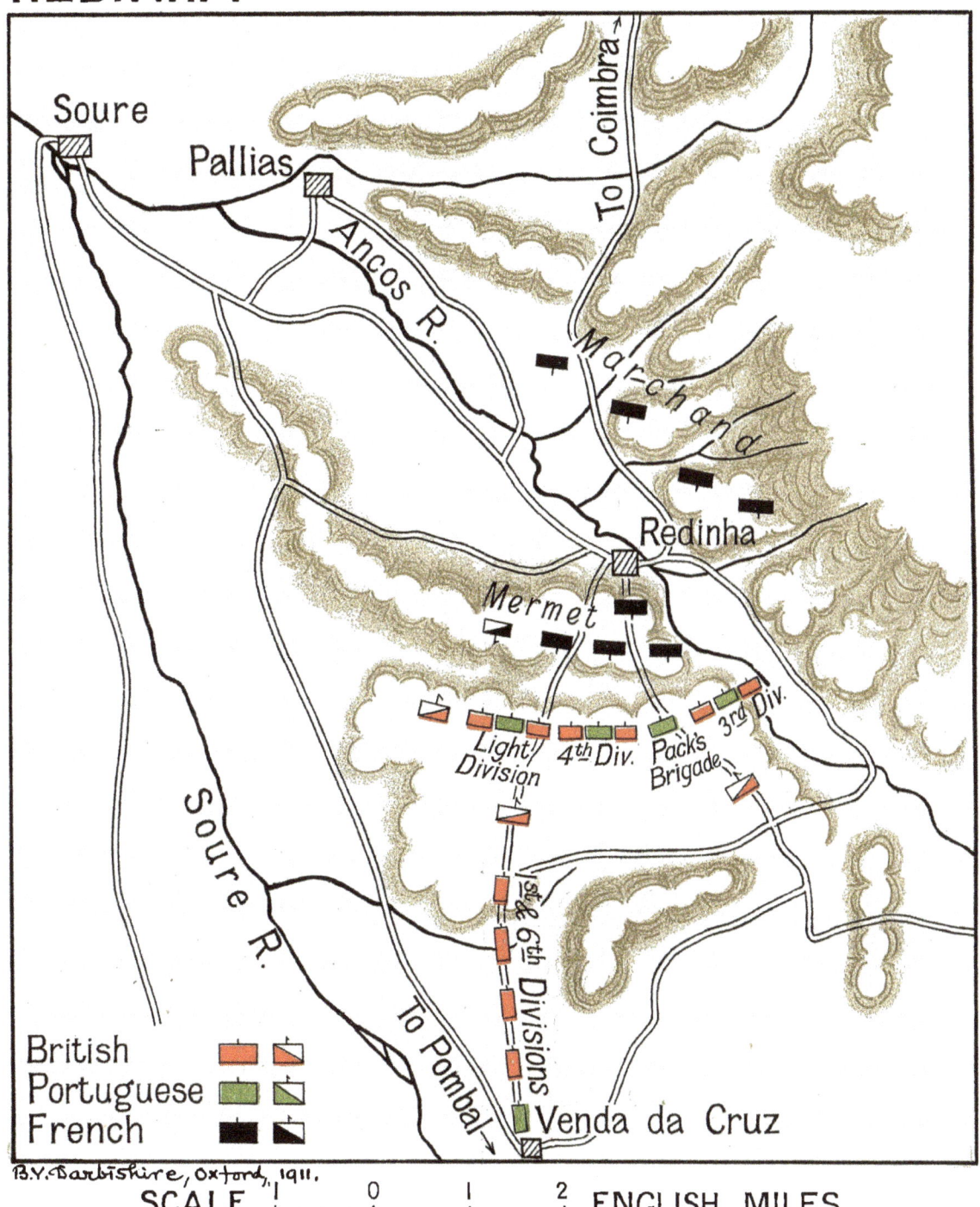

CASAL NOVO

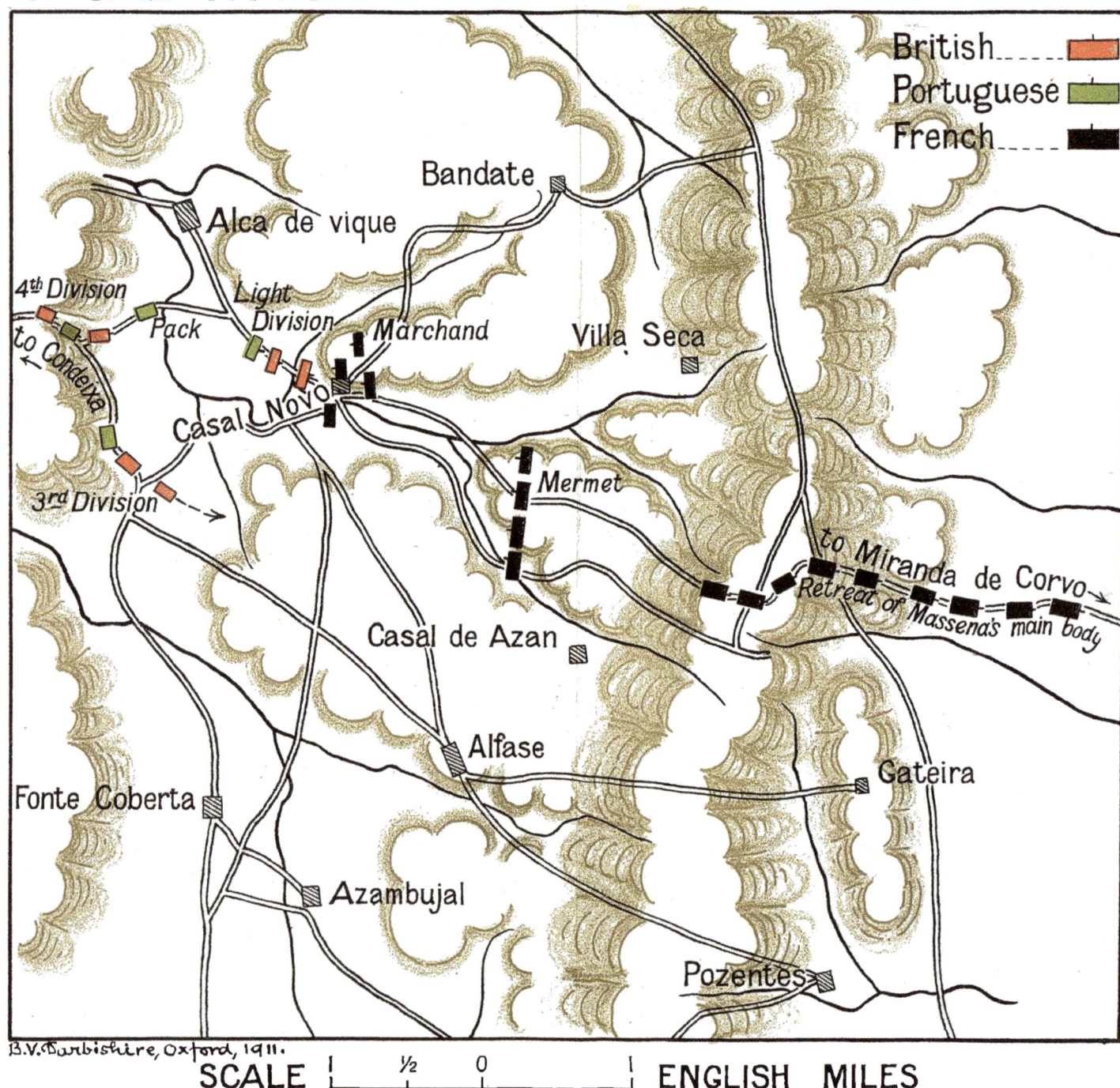

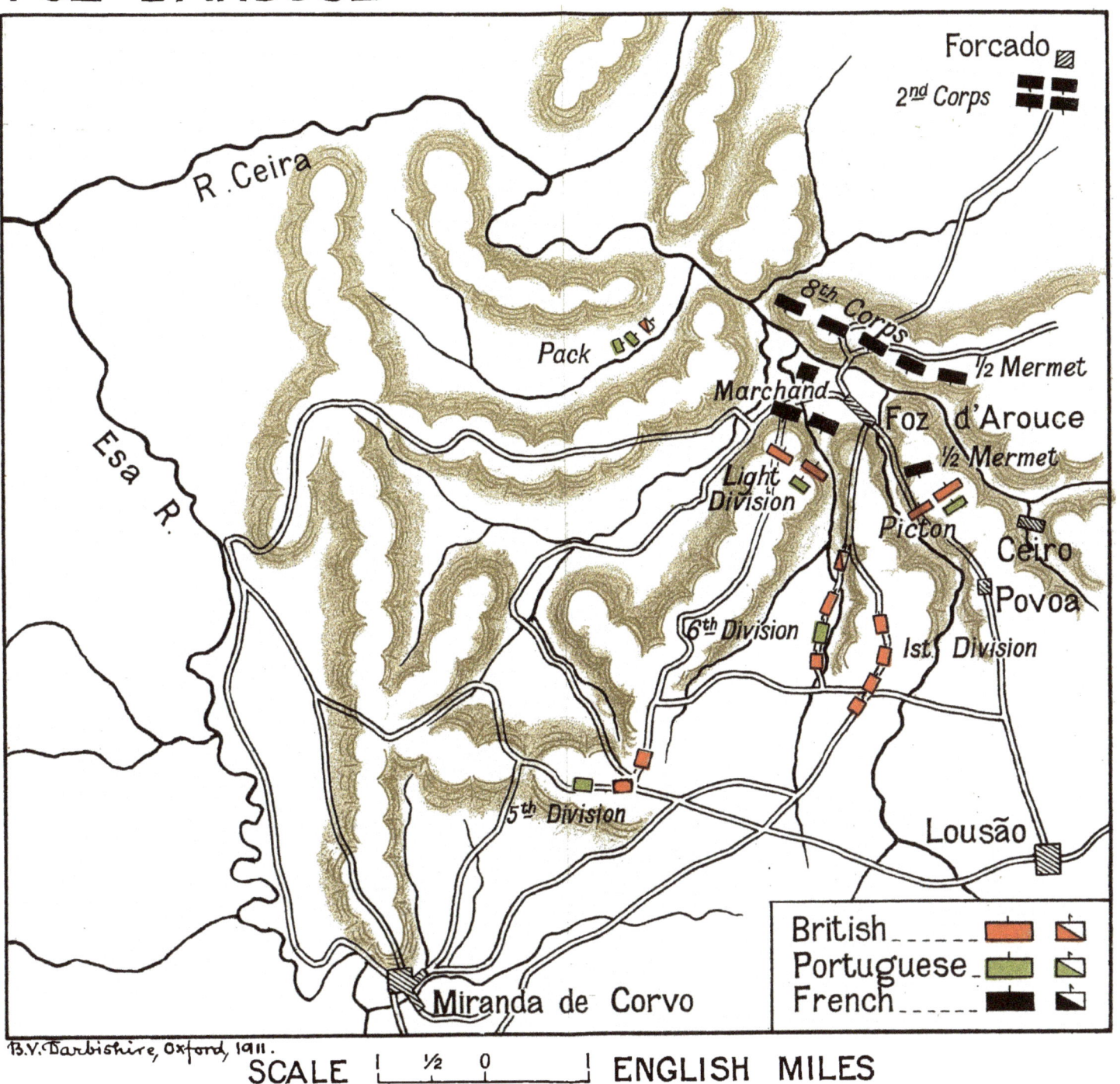

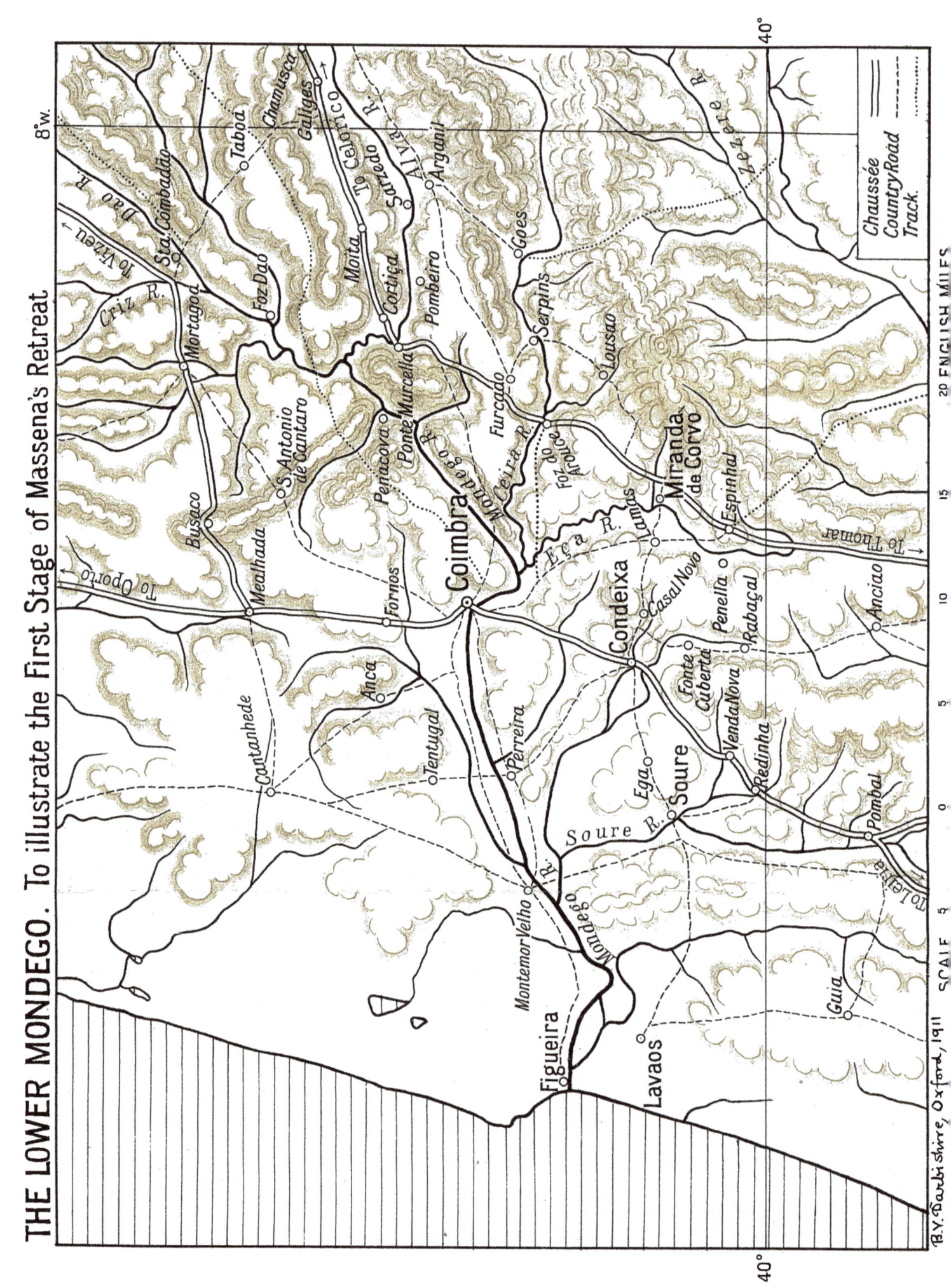

SABUGAL

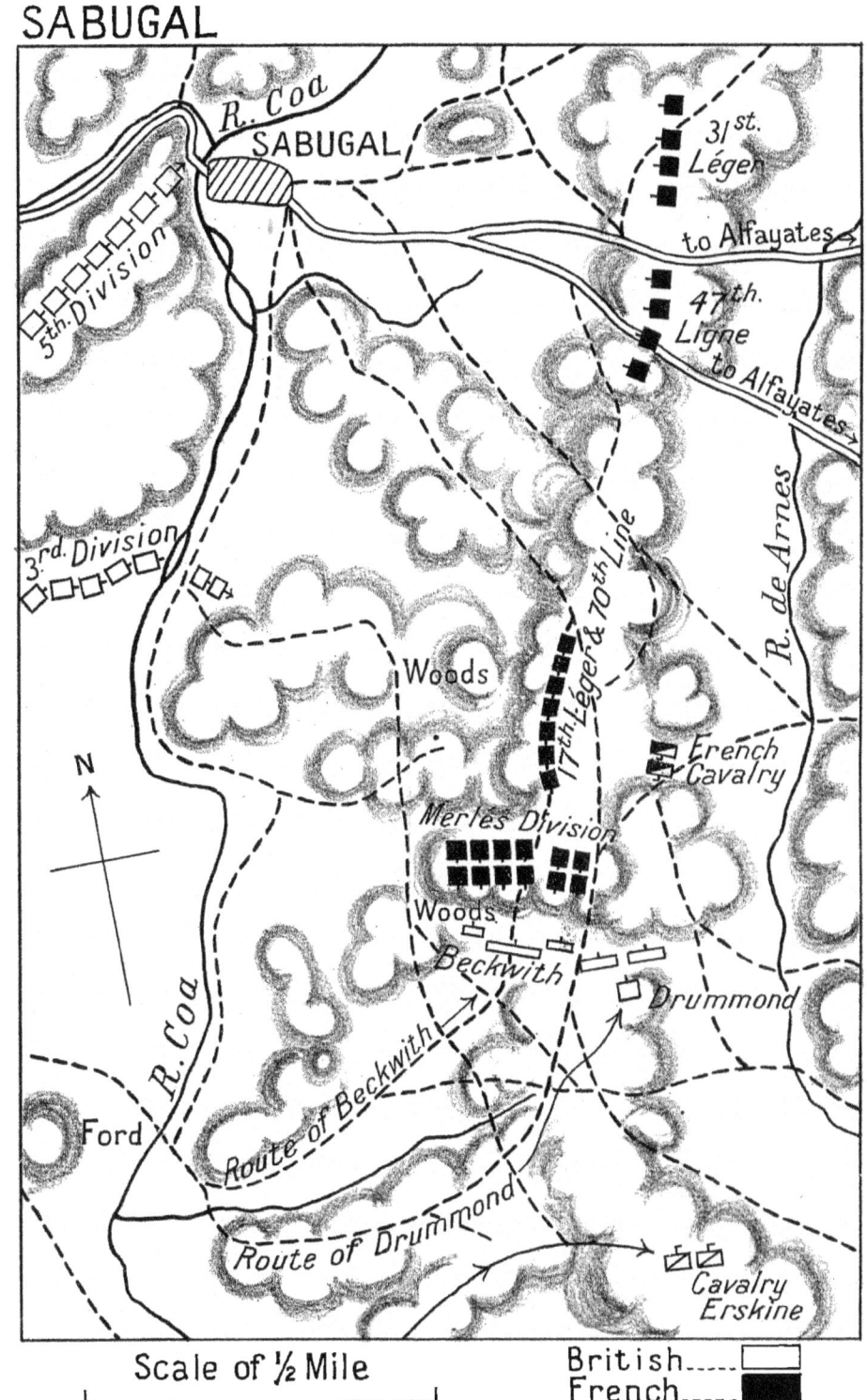

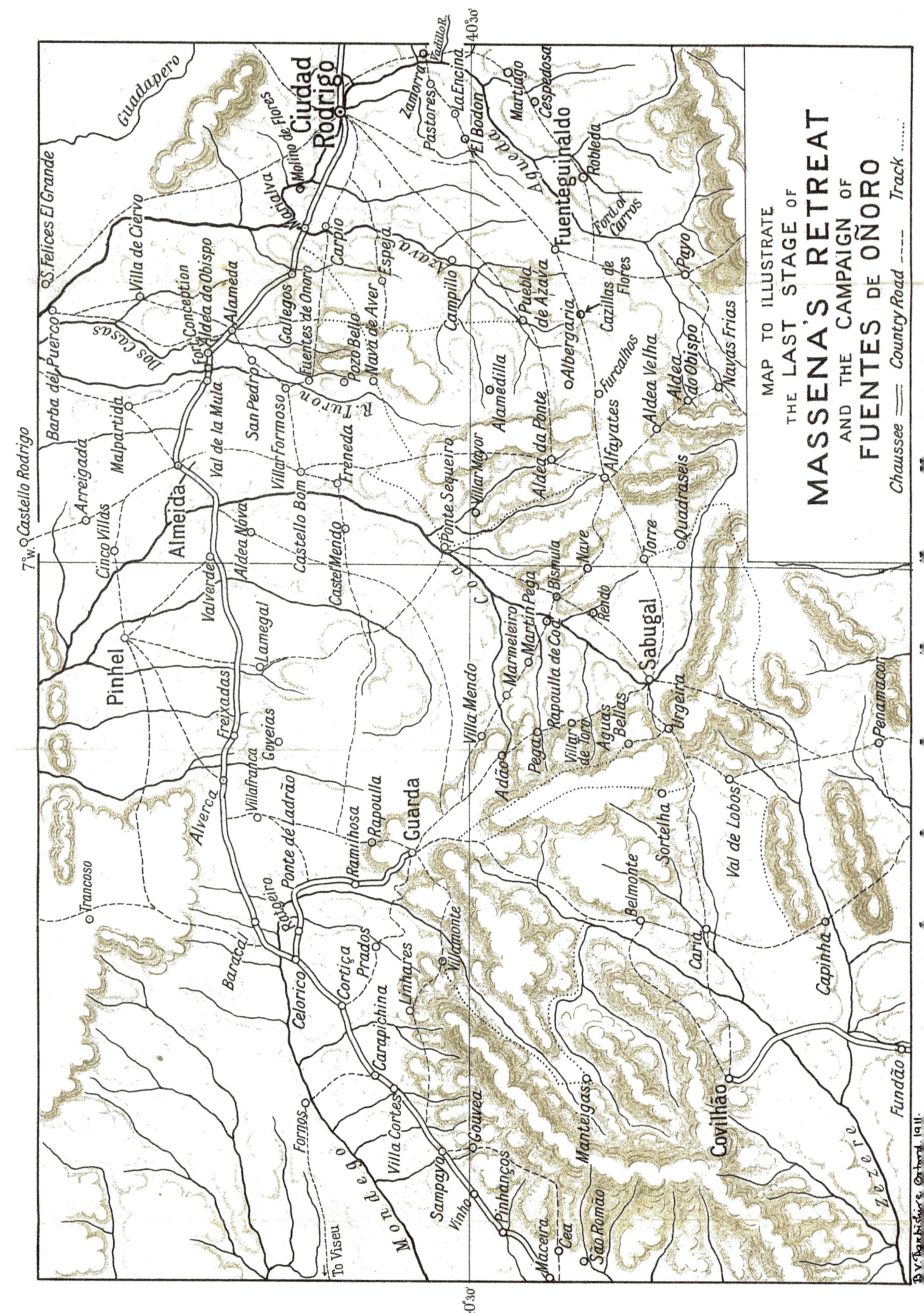

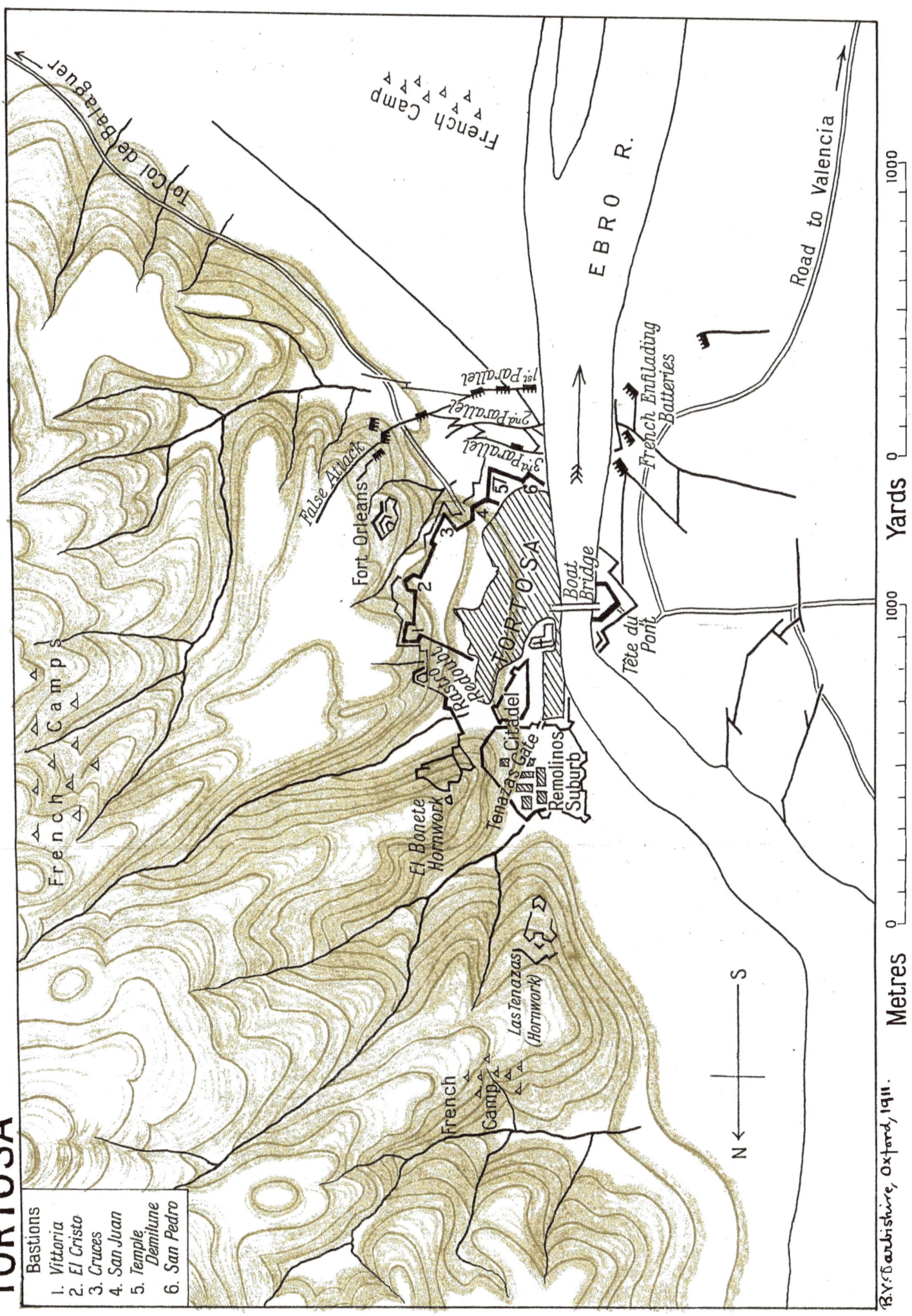

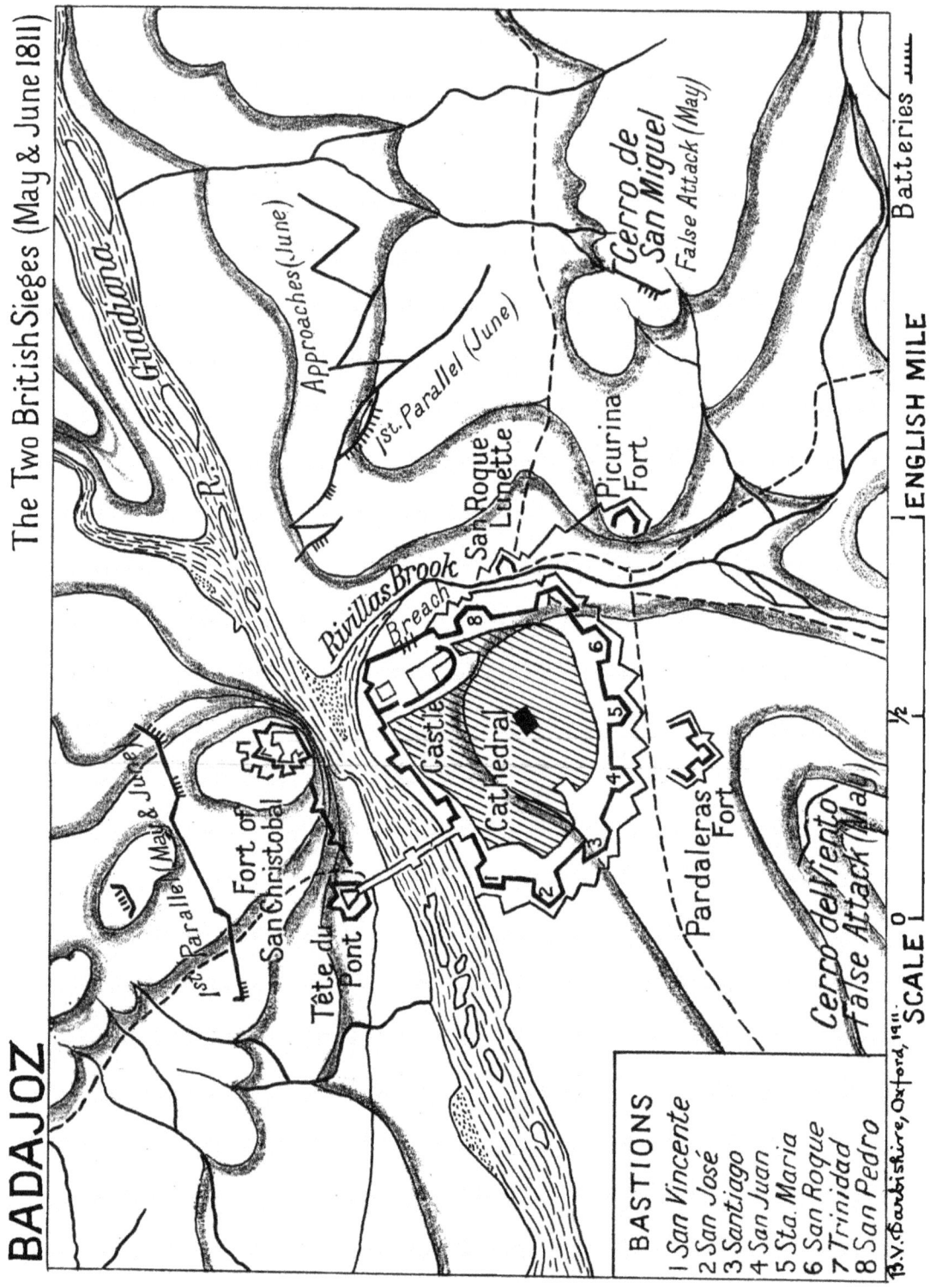

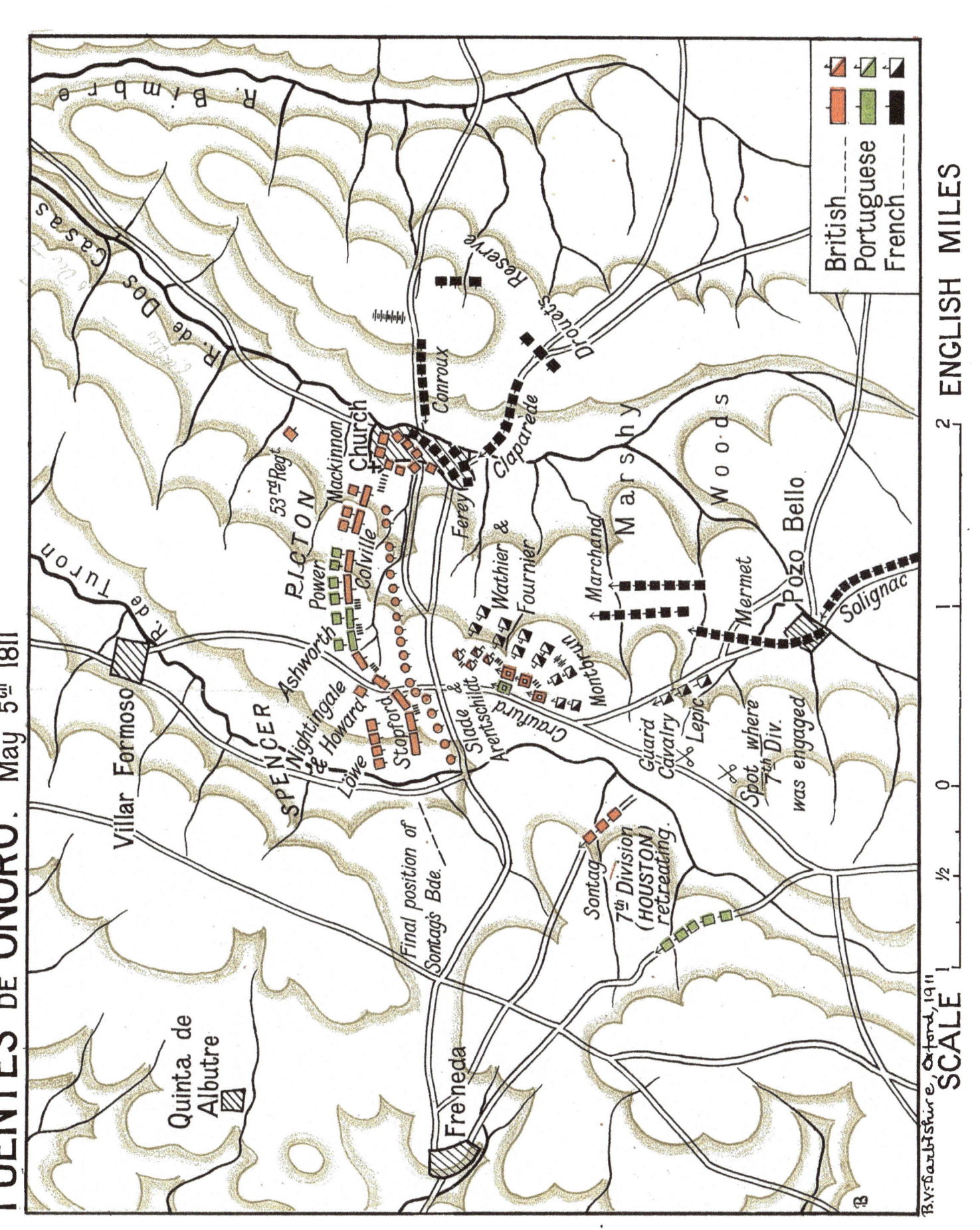

FUENTES DE OÑORO. Positions on the first day (May 3rd. 1811)

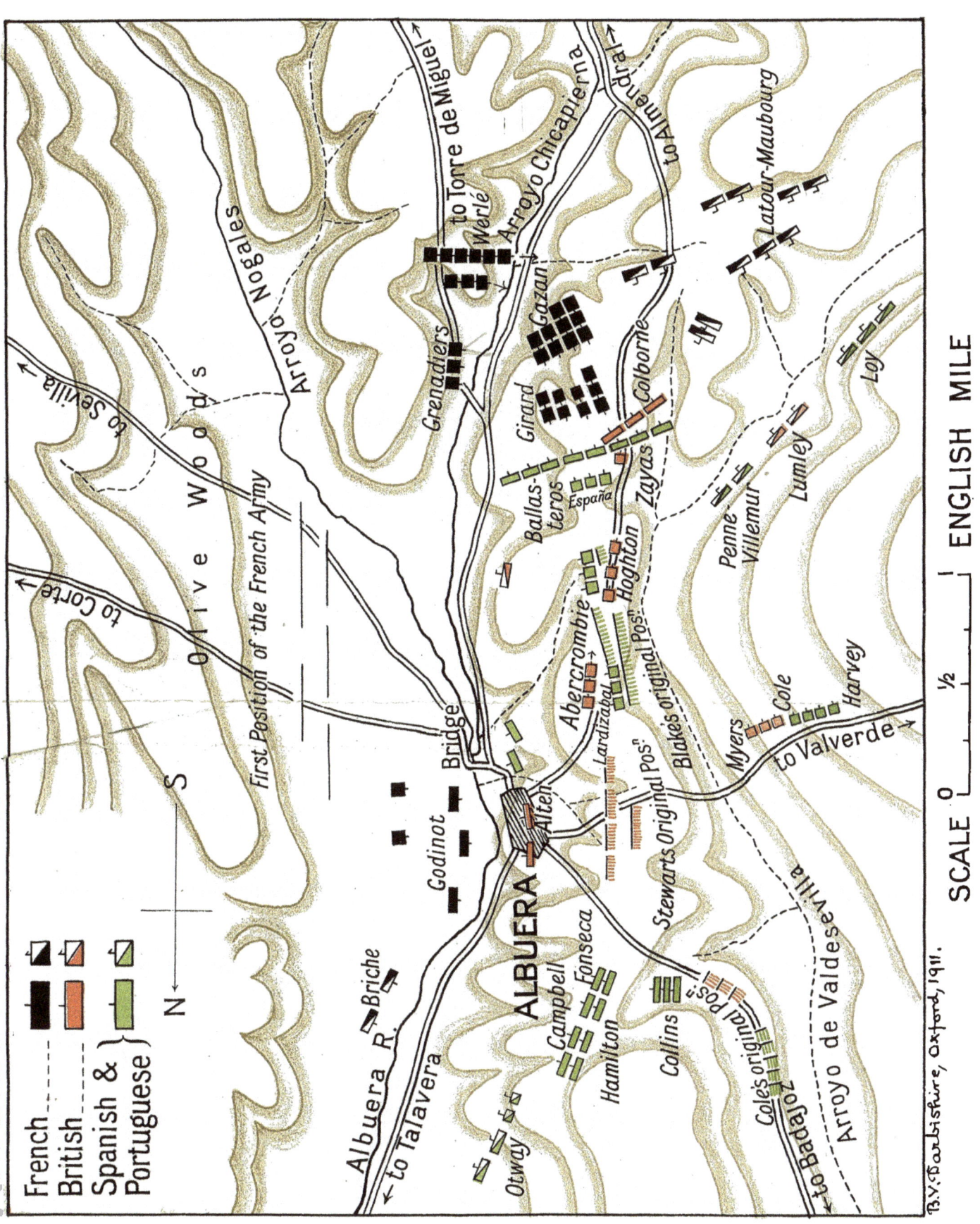

NOTE.—The front line of the French attacking force is not correctly represented. It consisted of a column of four battalions in the centre, flanked by two deployed battalions, and with battalions in column placed outside the two deployed battalions on either side (see p. 380). In the French reserve there should be only two, not three, battalions of Grenadiers. The right flank of Zayas's line is two battalions too long.

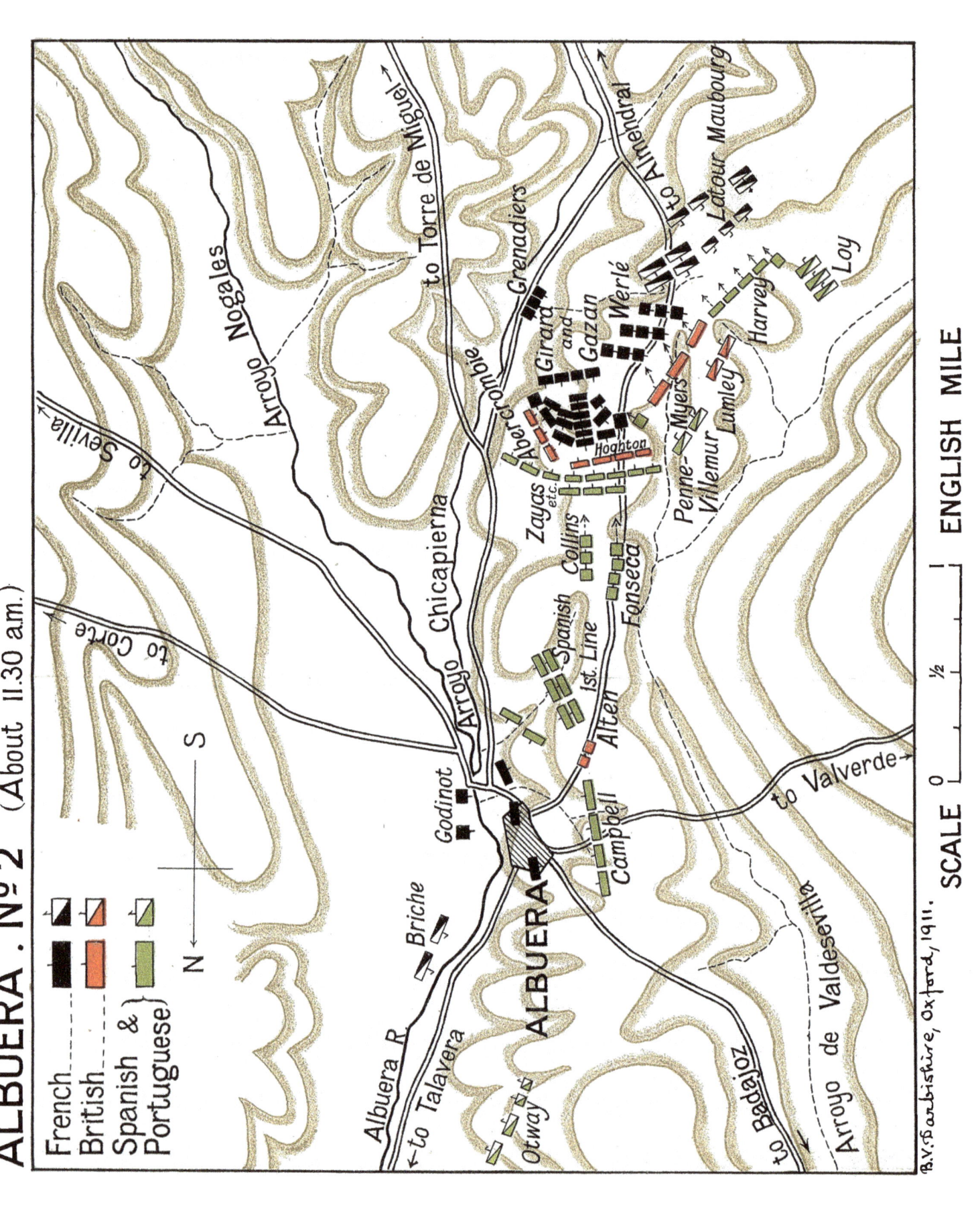

TARRAGONA

CATALONIA

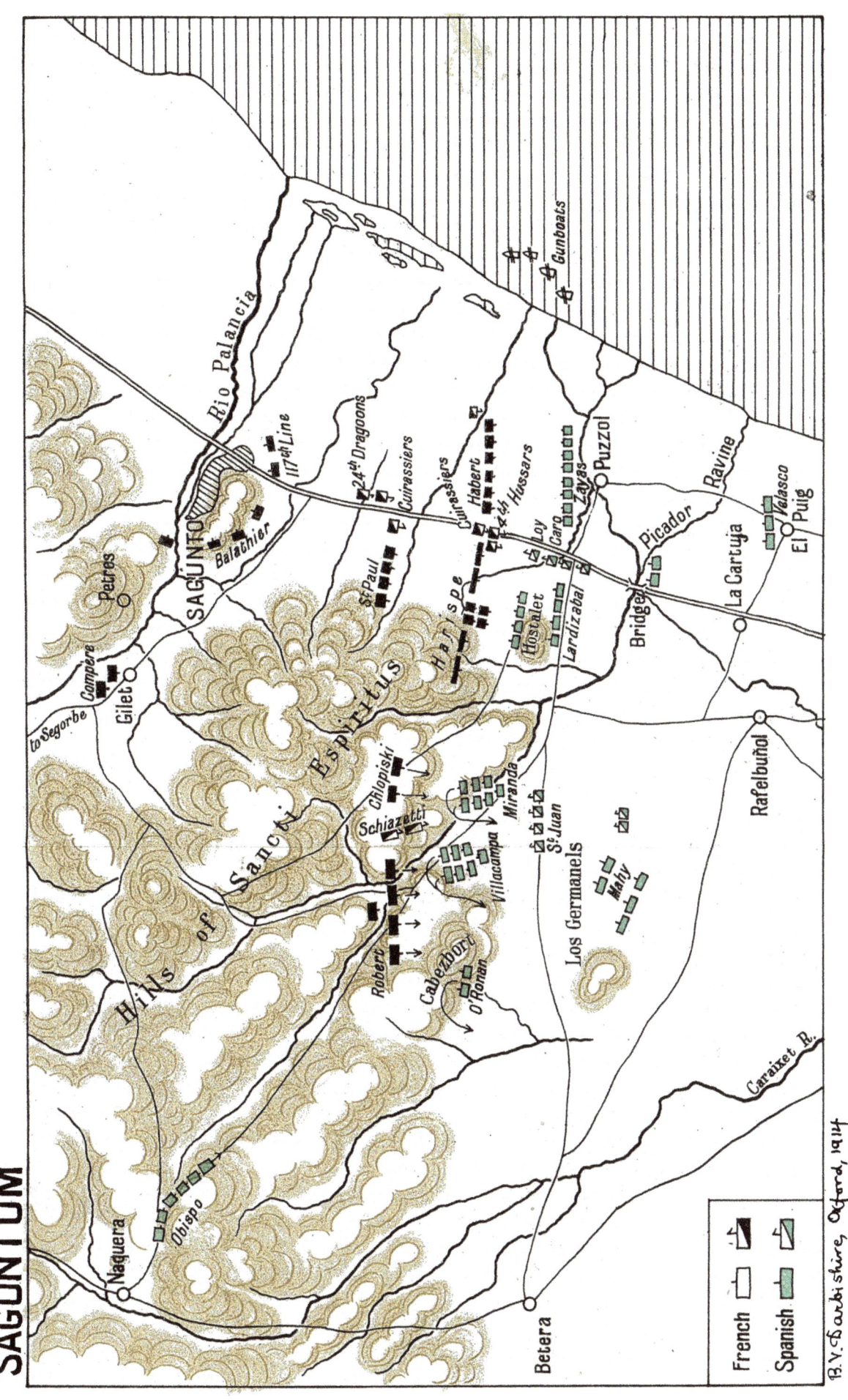

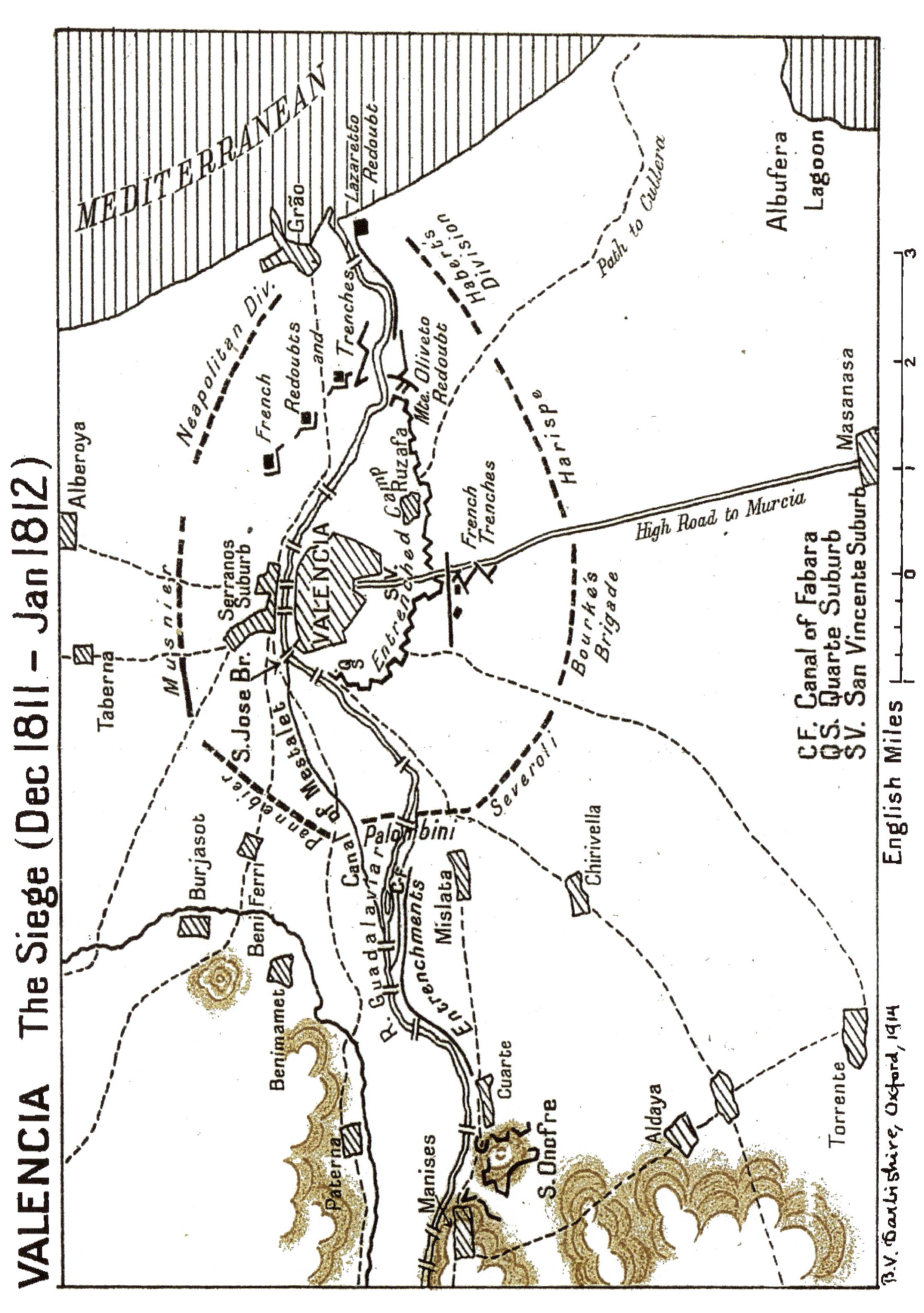

CATALONIA

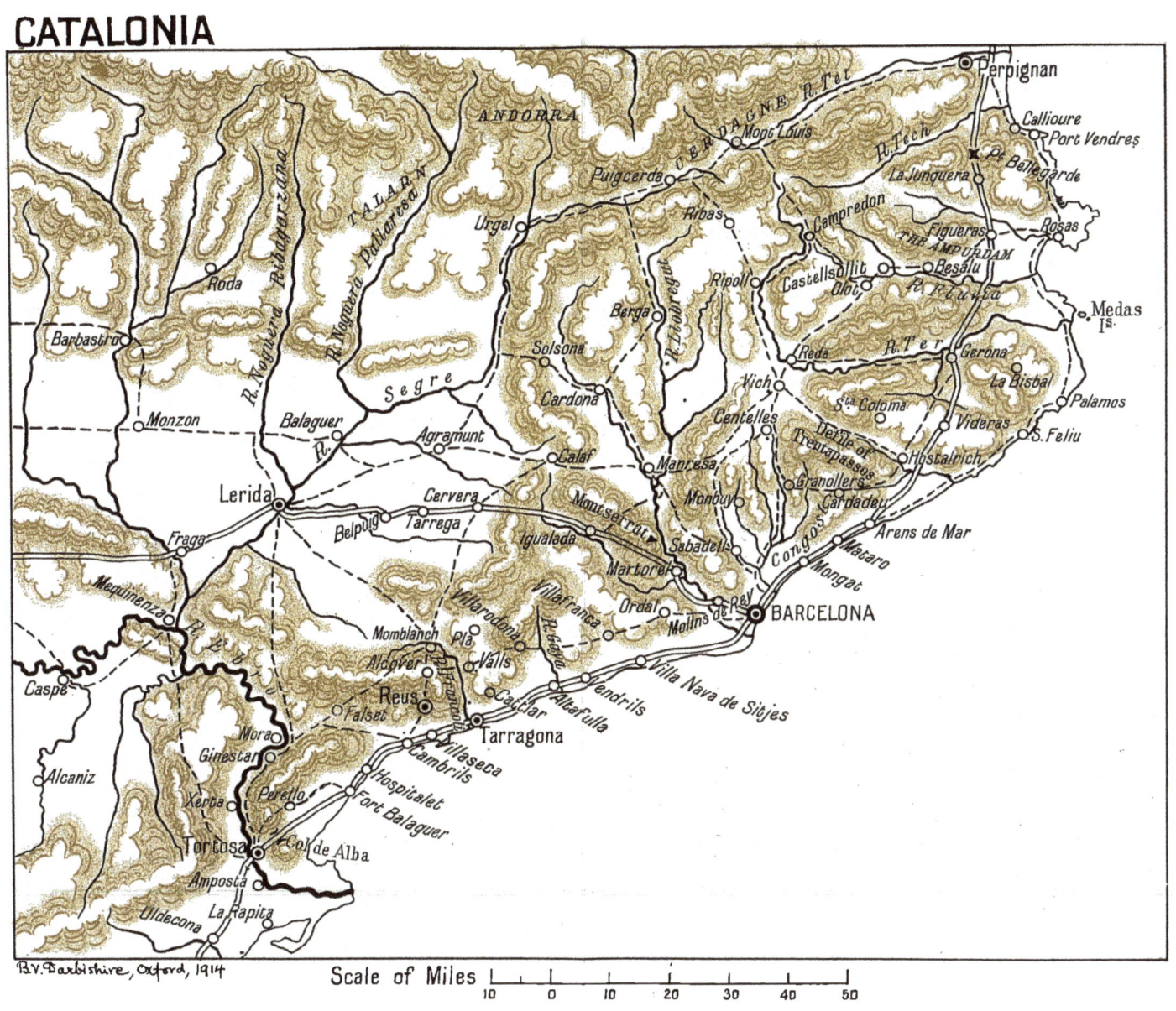

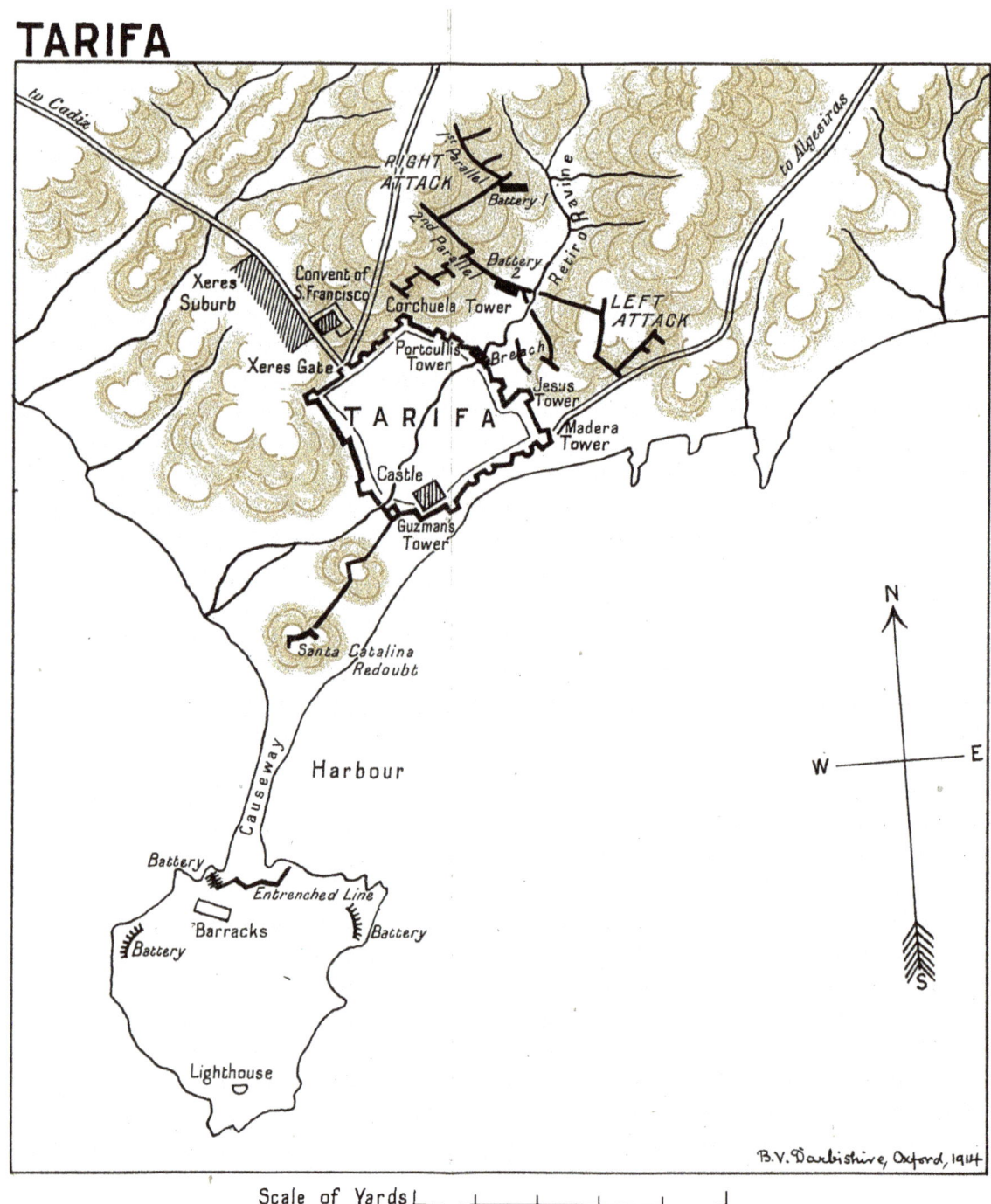

CIUDAD RODRIGO

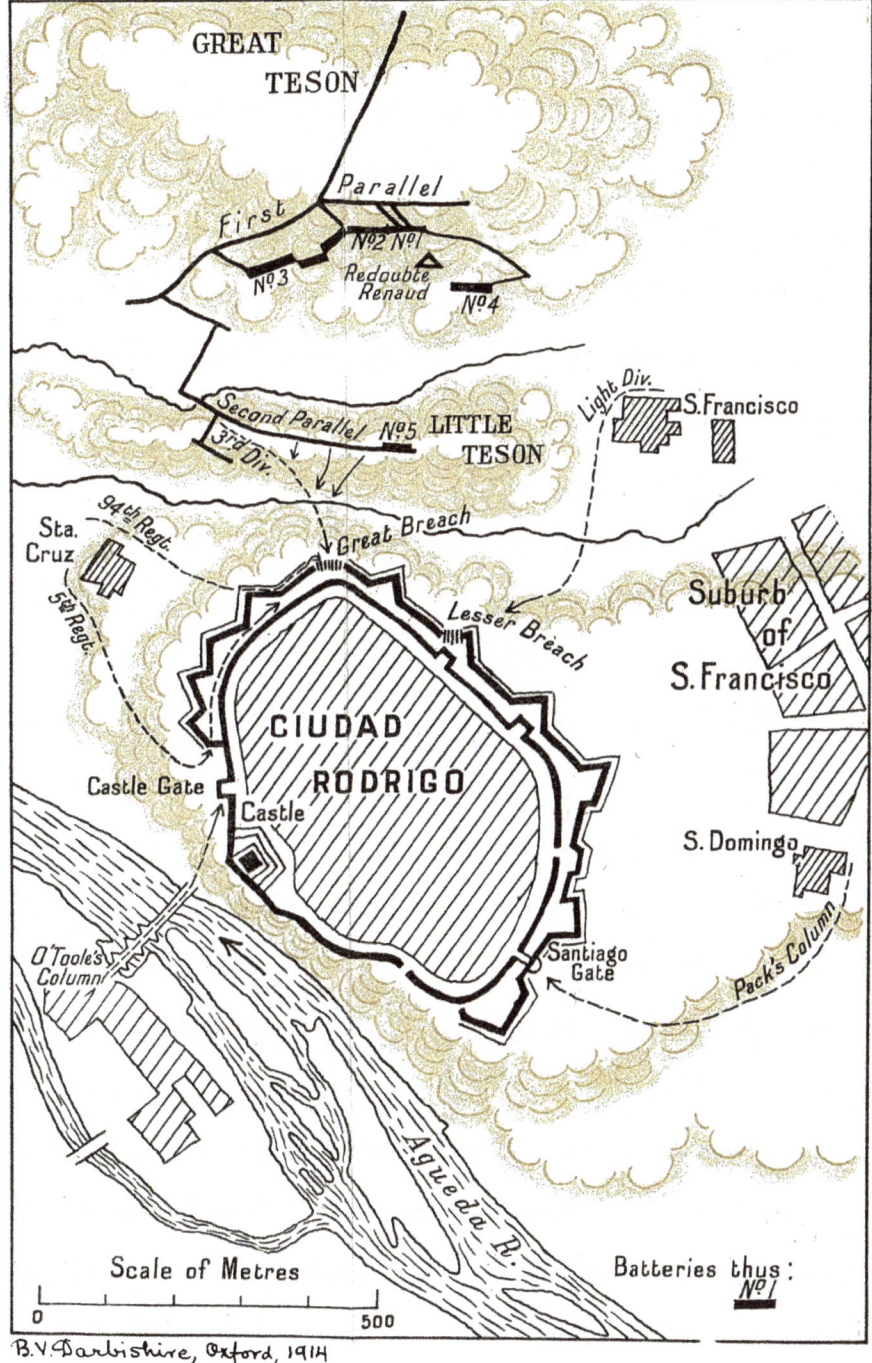

BADAJOZ

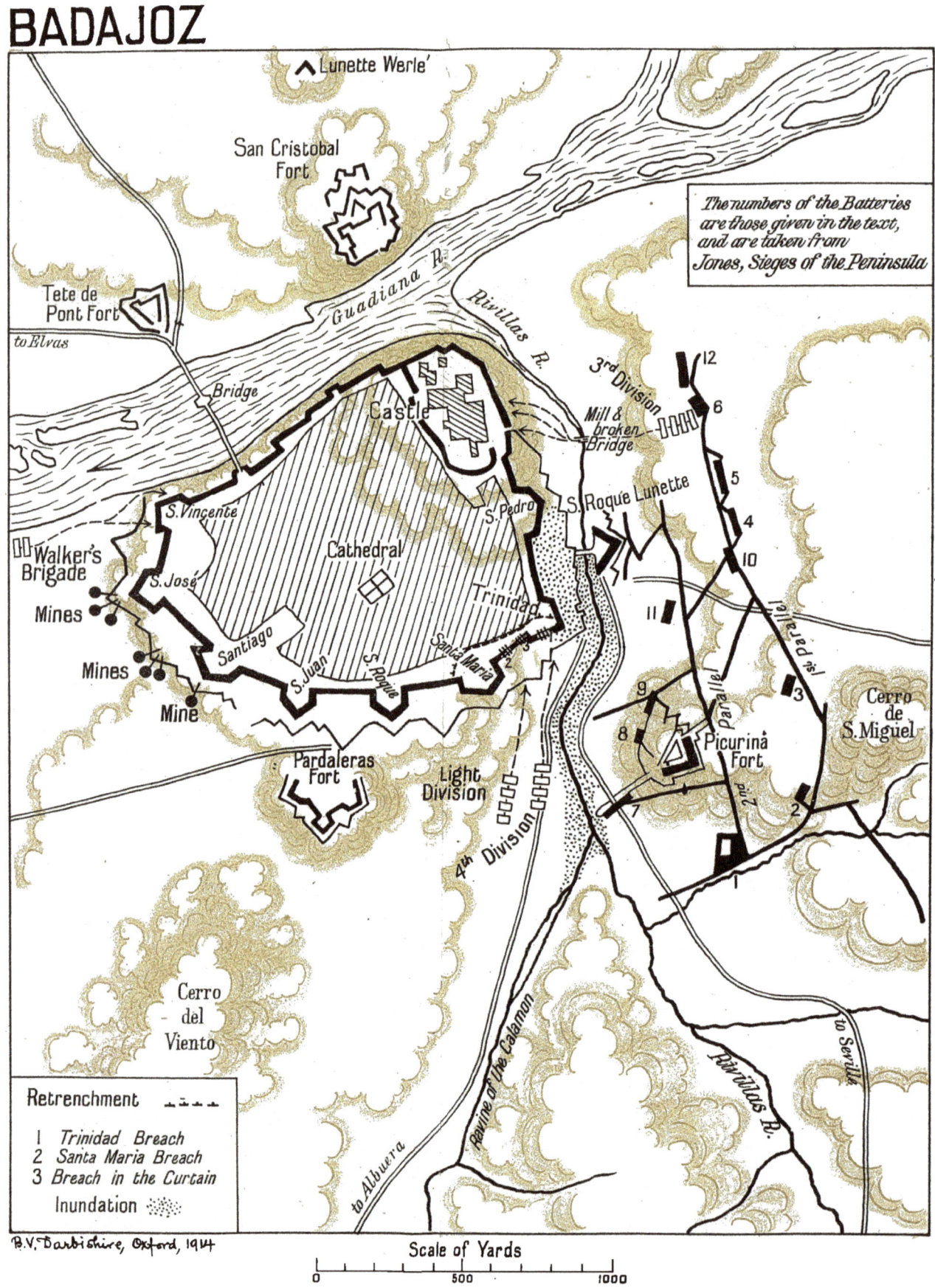

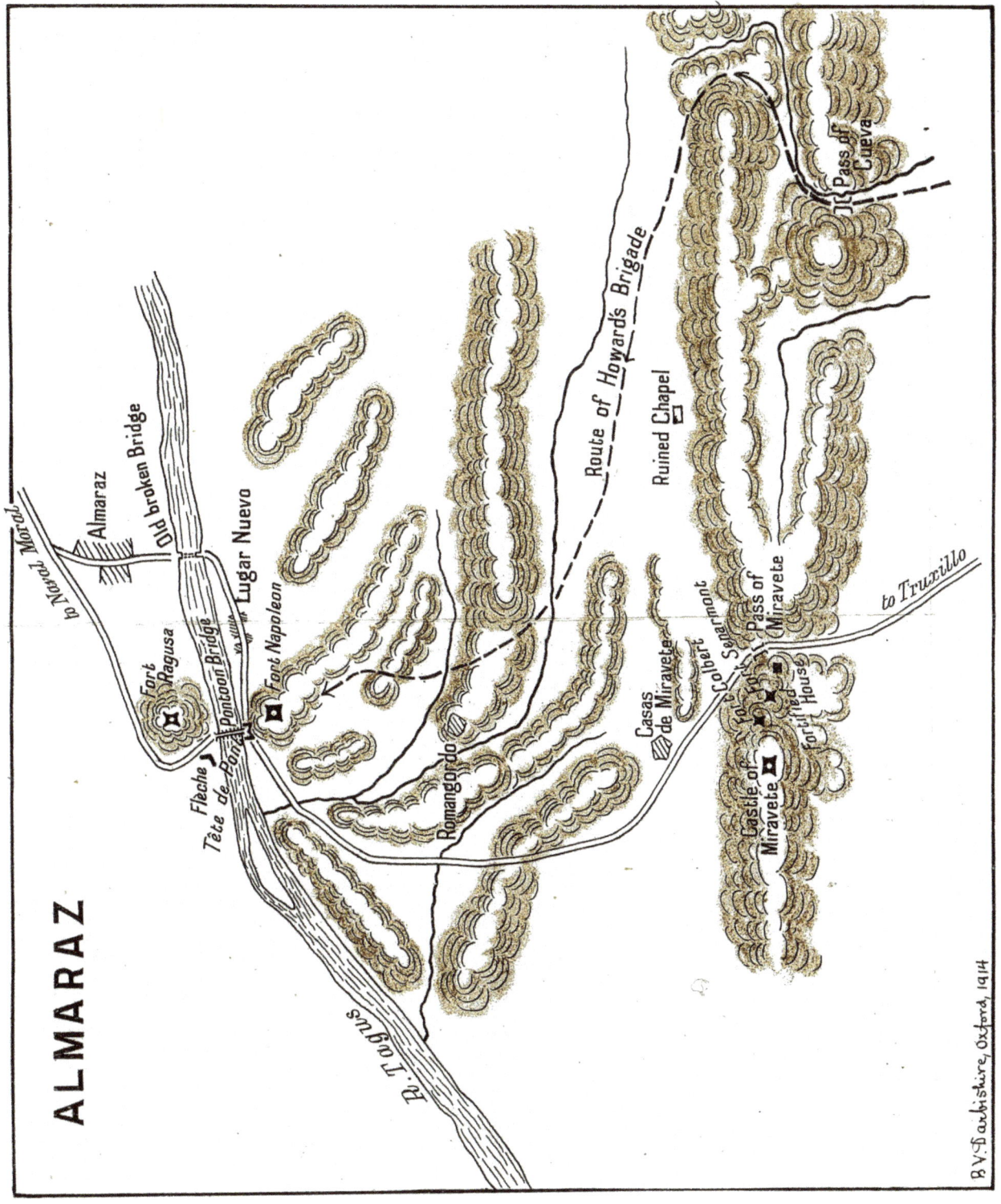

CENTRAL SPAIN

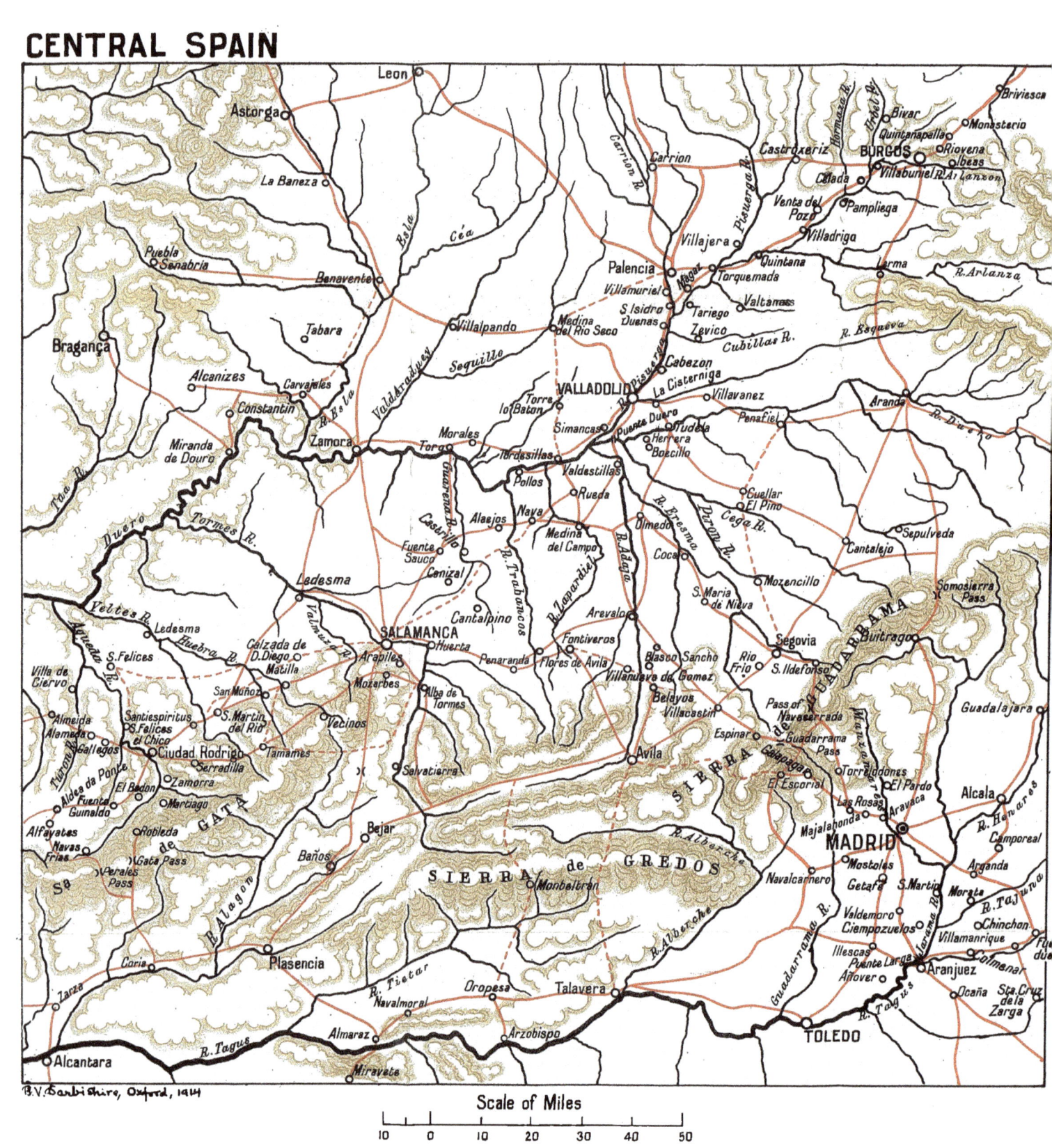

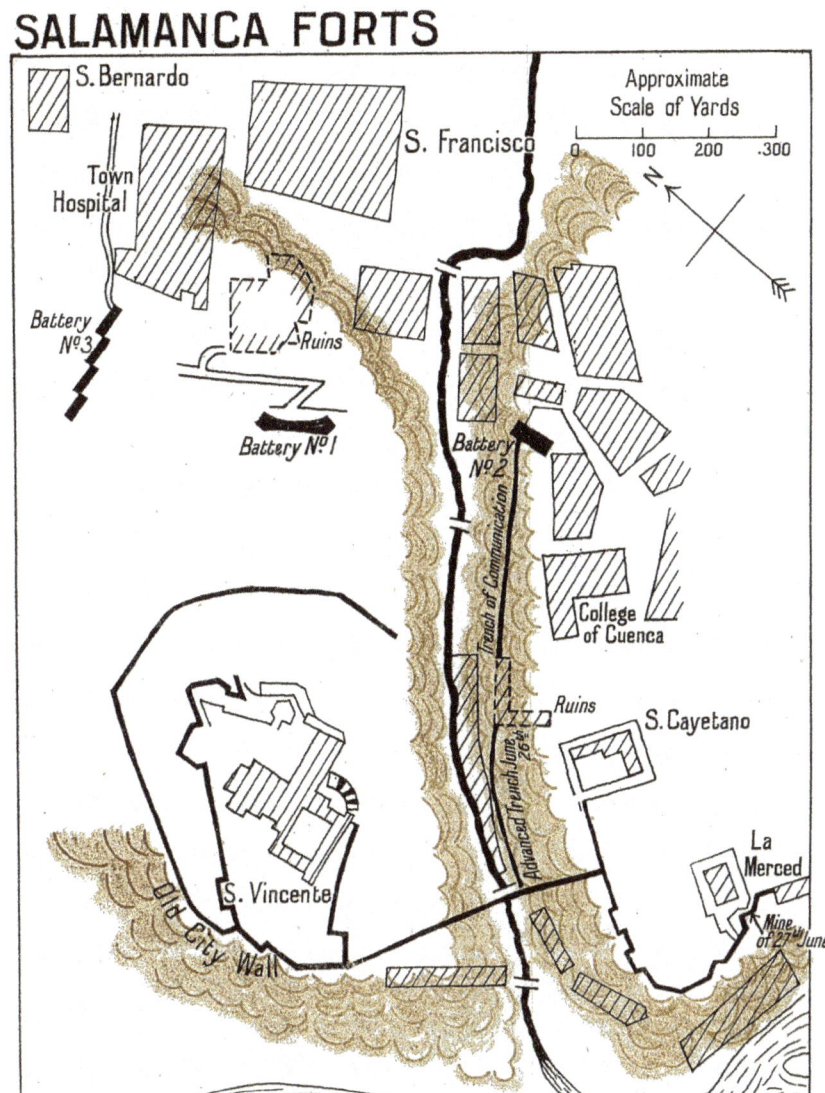

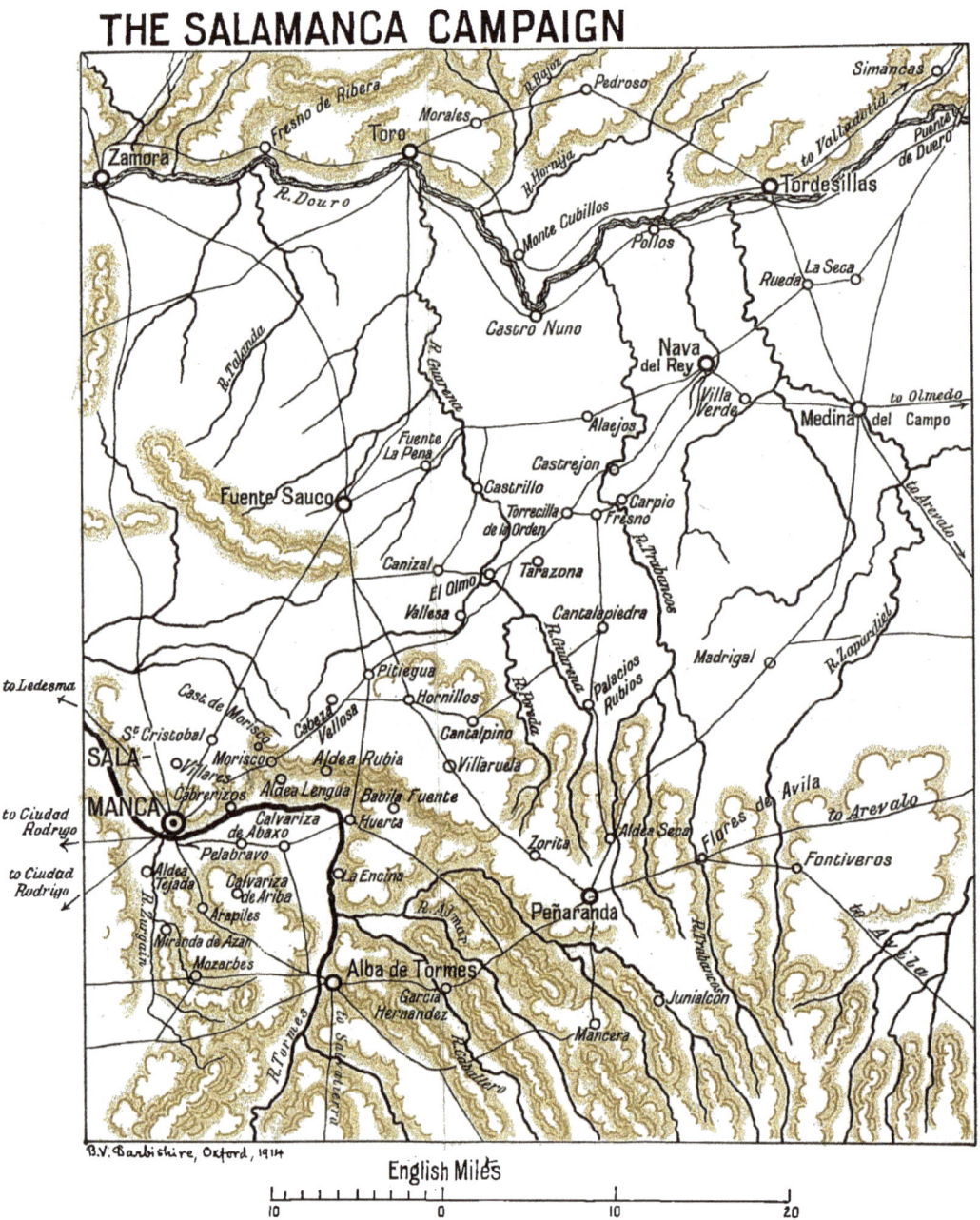

SALAMANCA

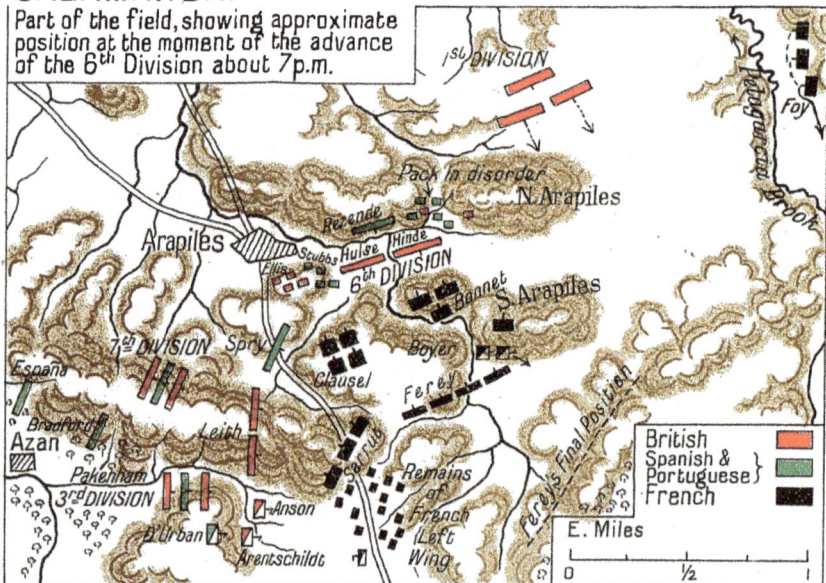

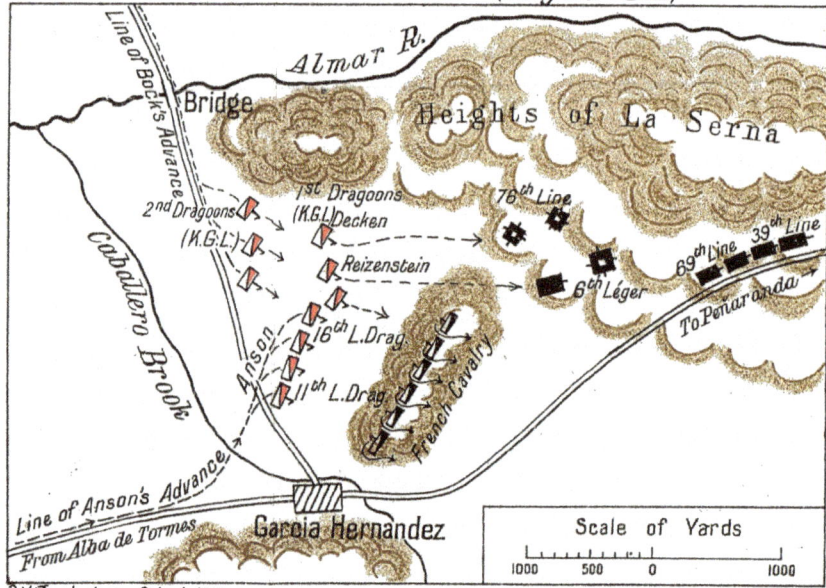

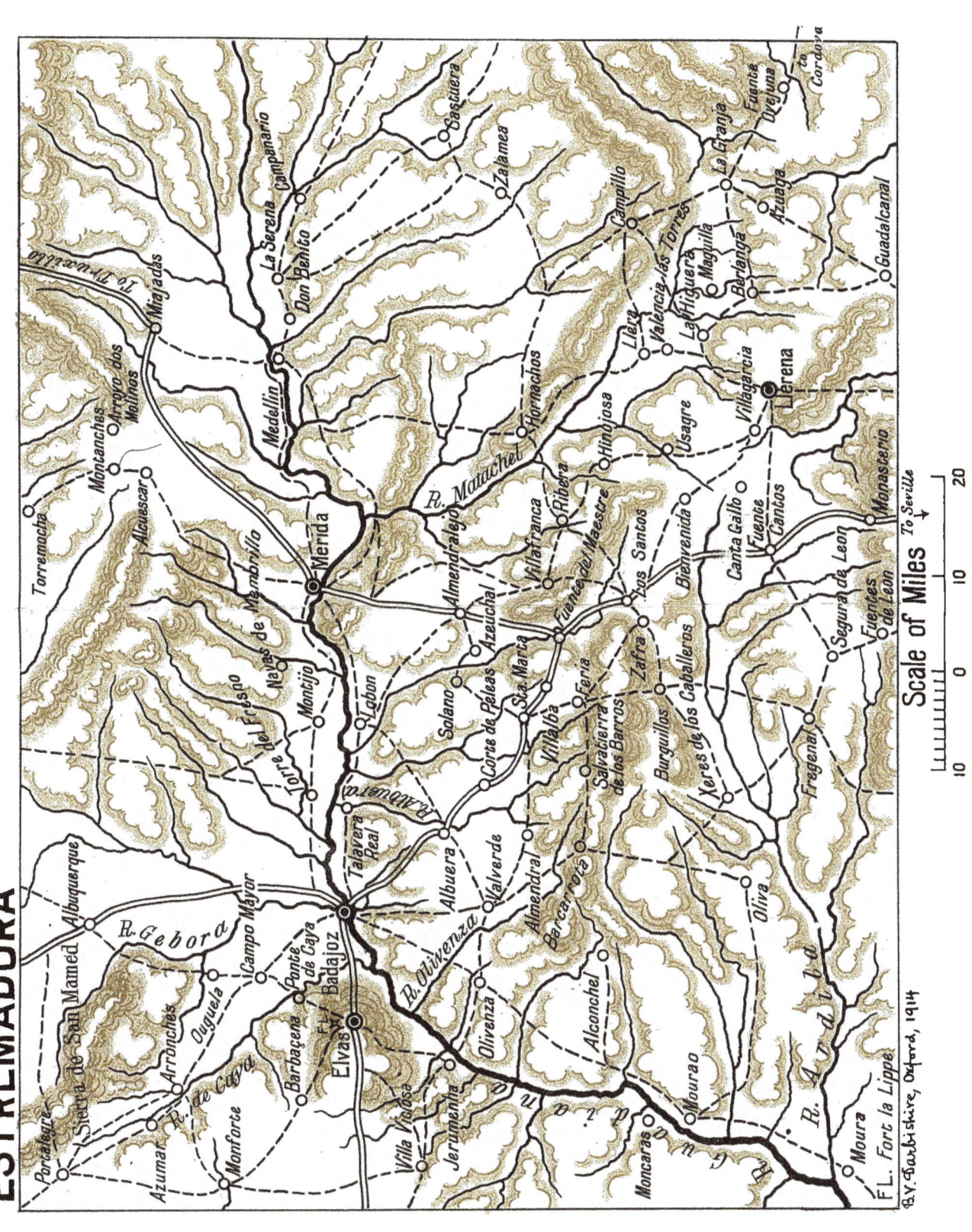

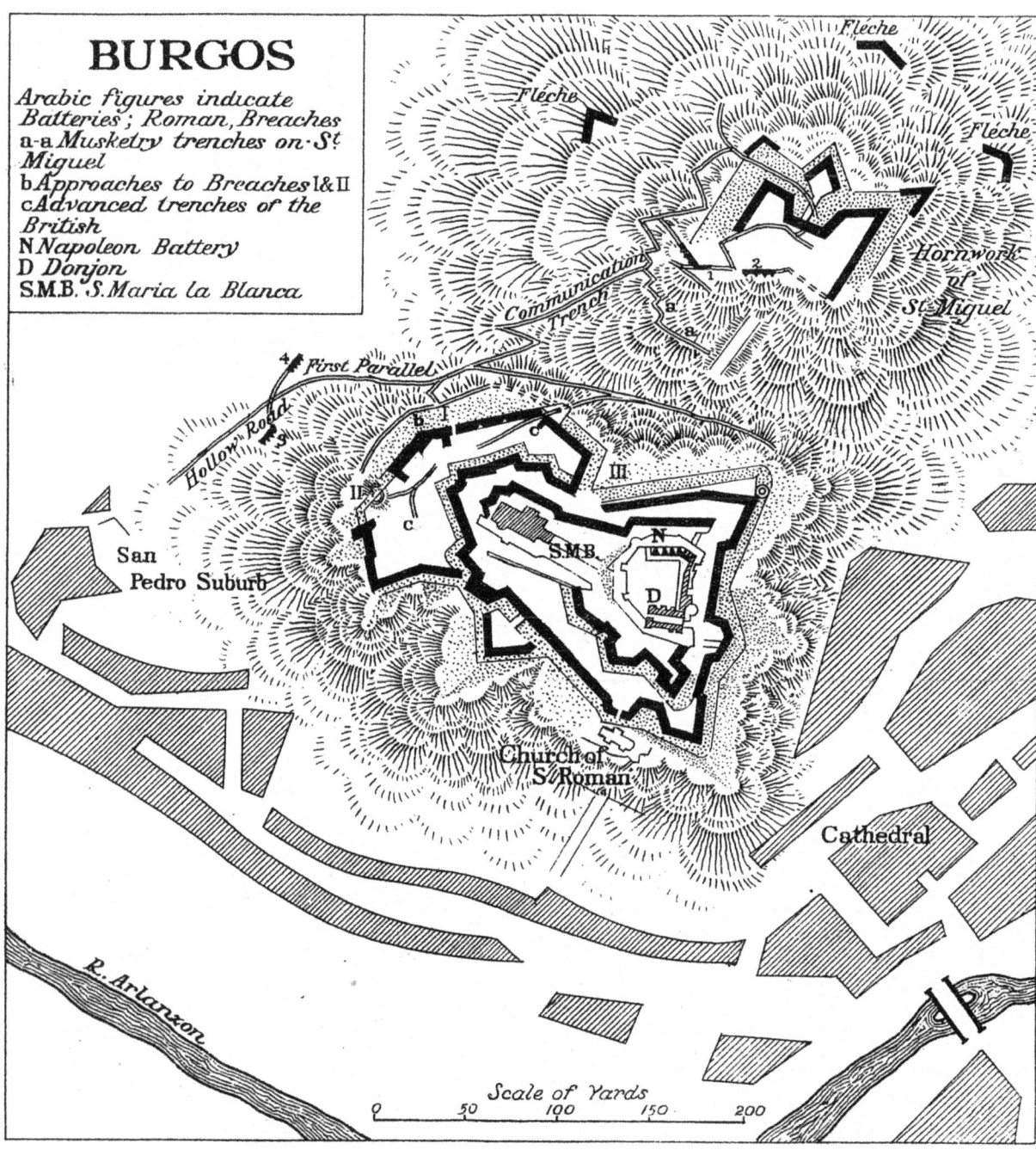

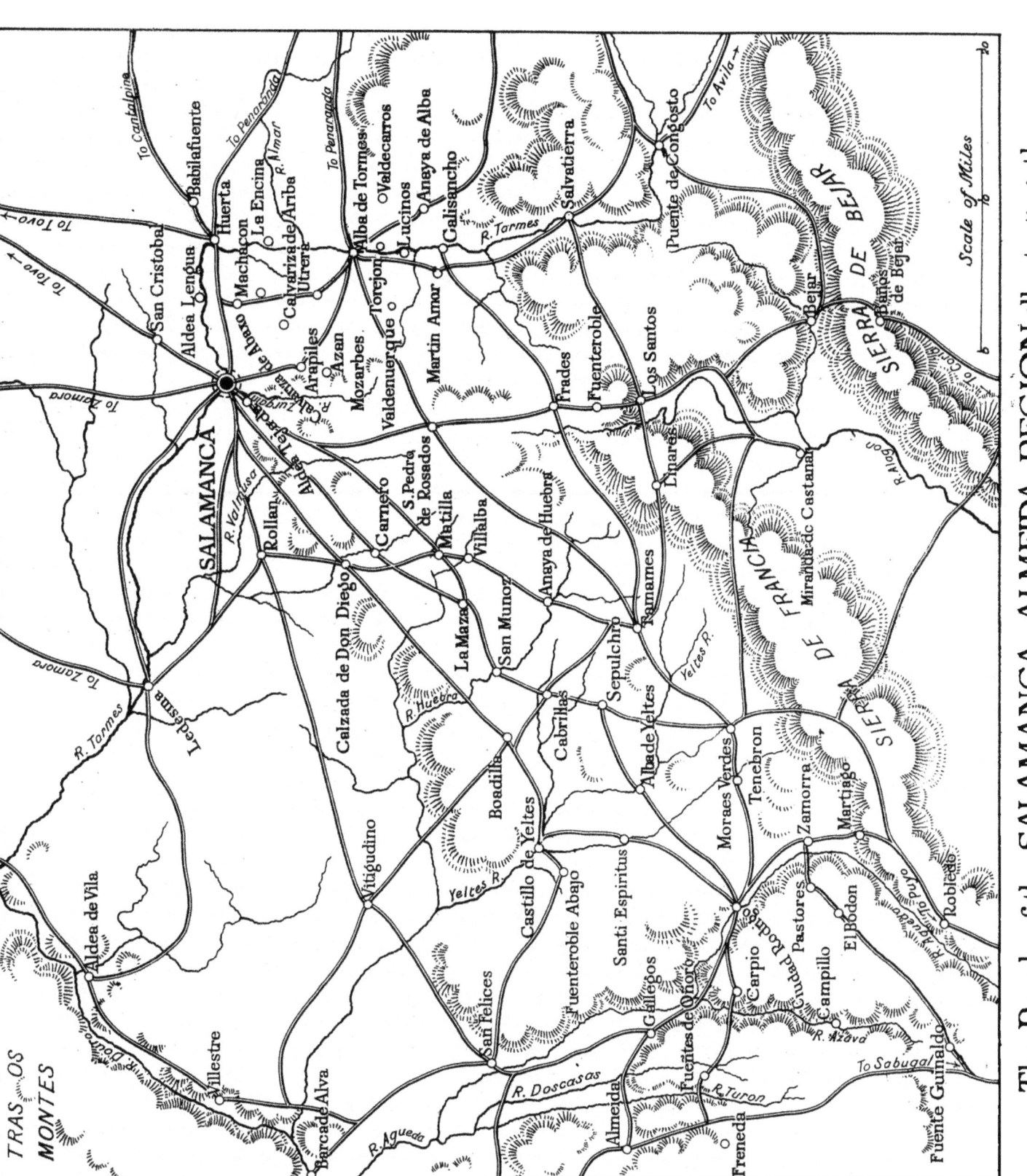

The Roads of the SALAMANCA ALMEIDA REGION illustrating the SALAMANCA Retreat of November 1812

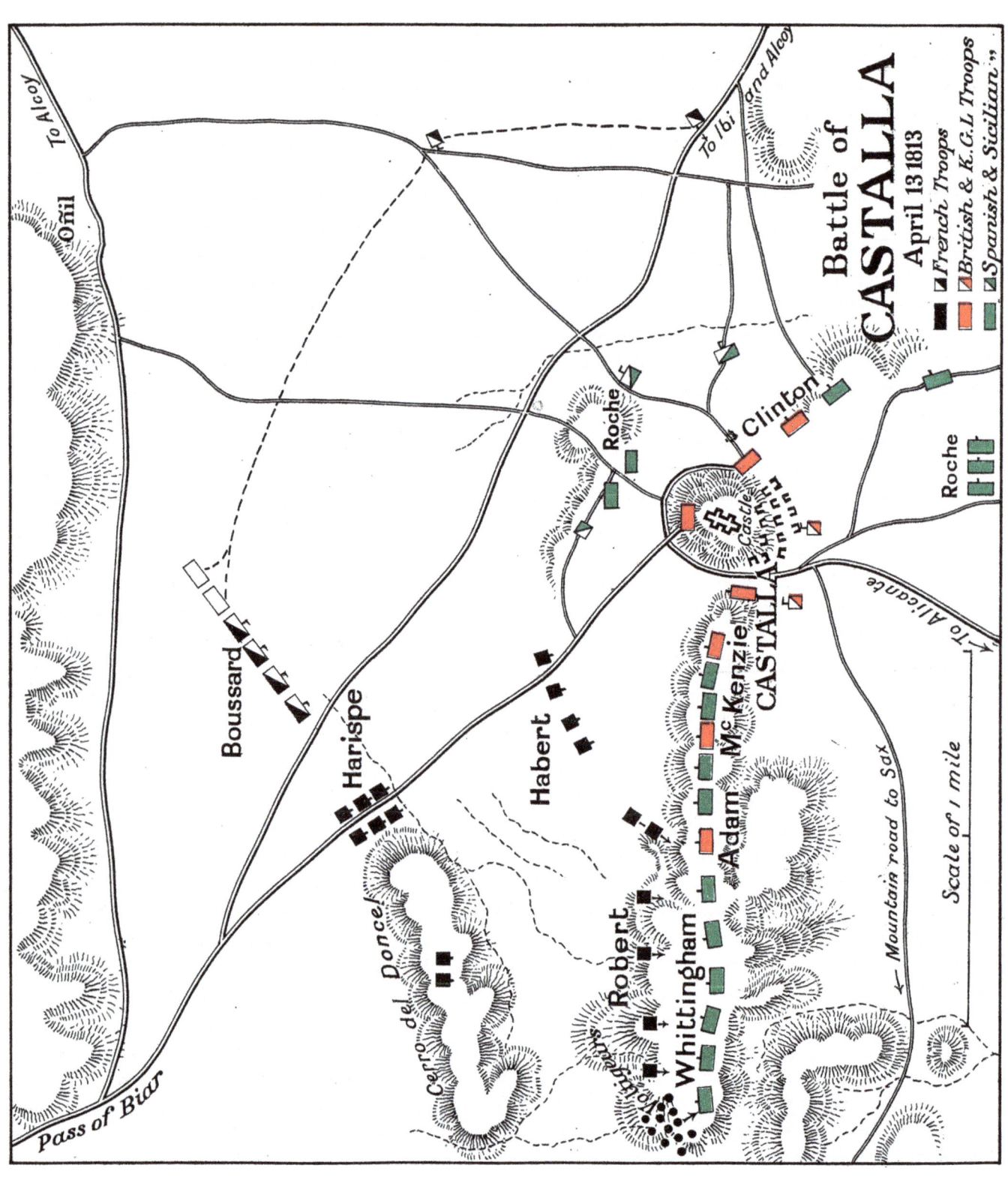

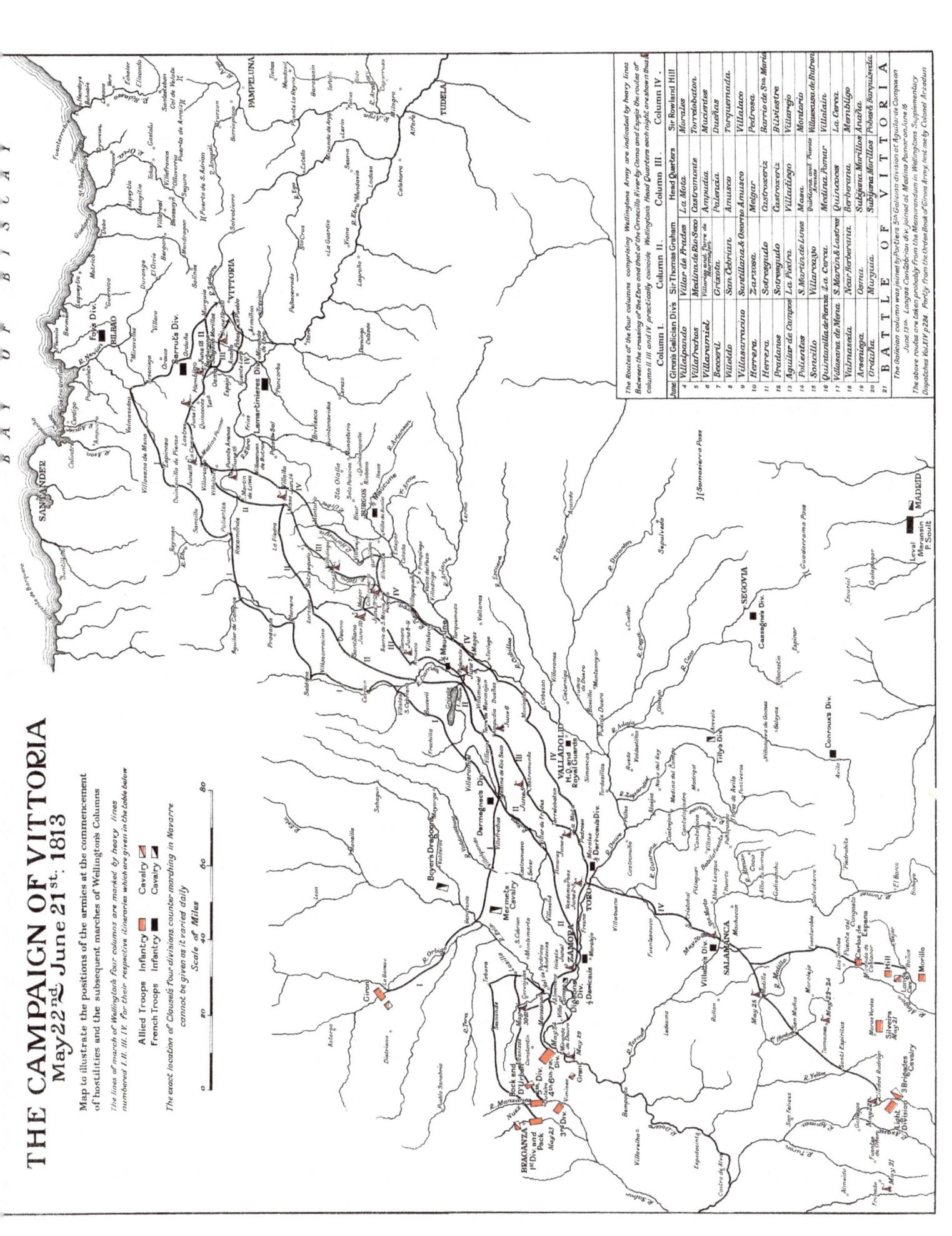

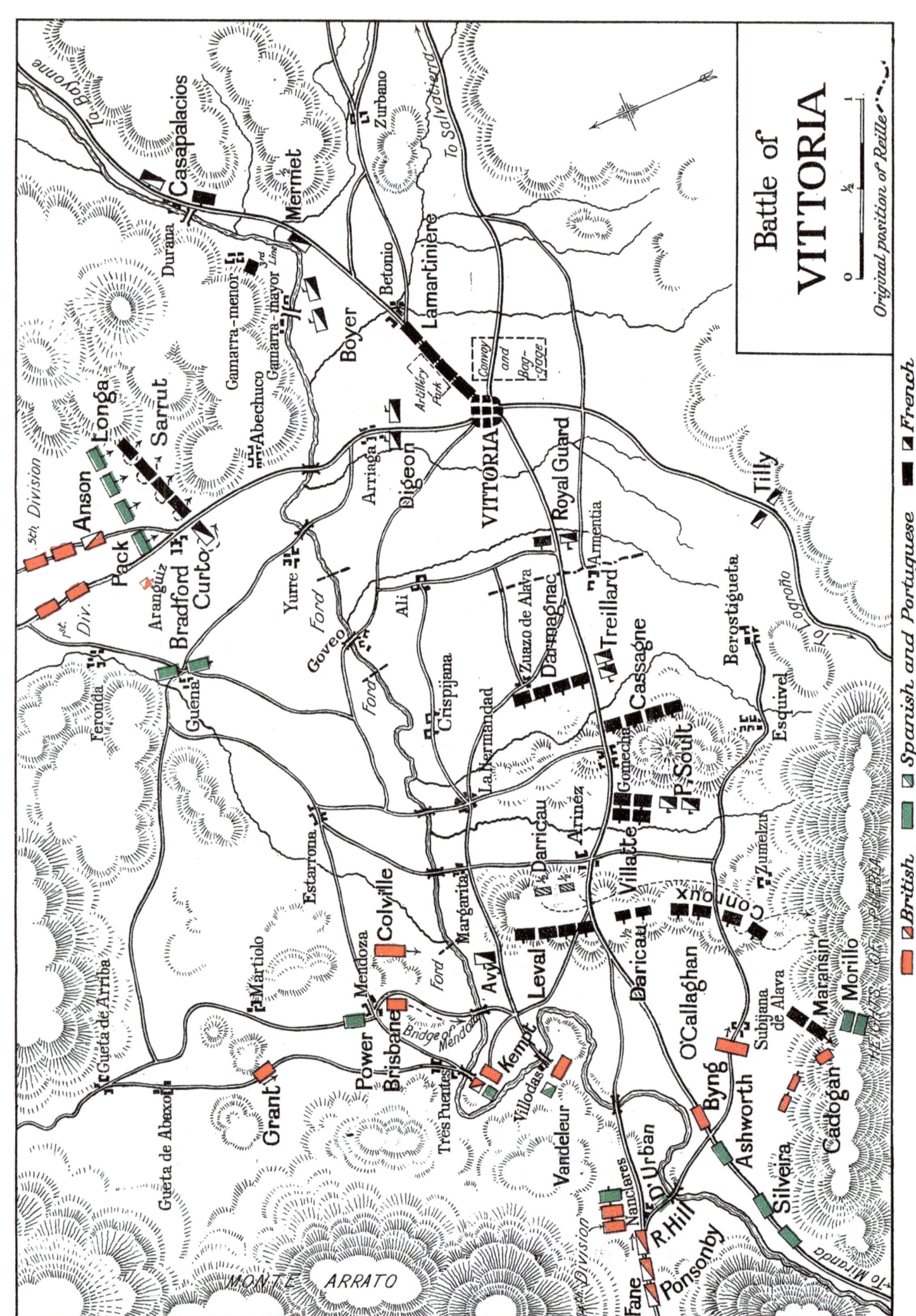

Attack of St. SEBASTIAN between 11th July & 9th Sept 1813

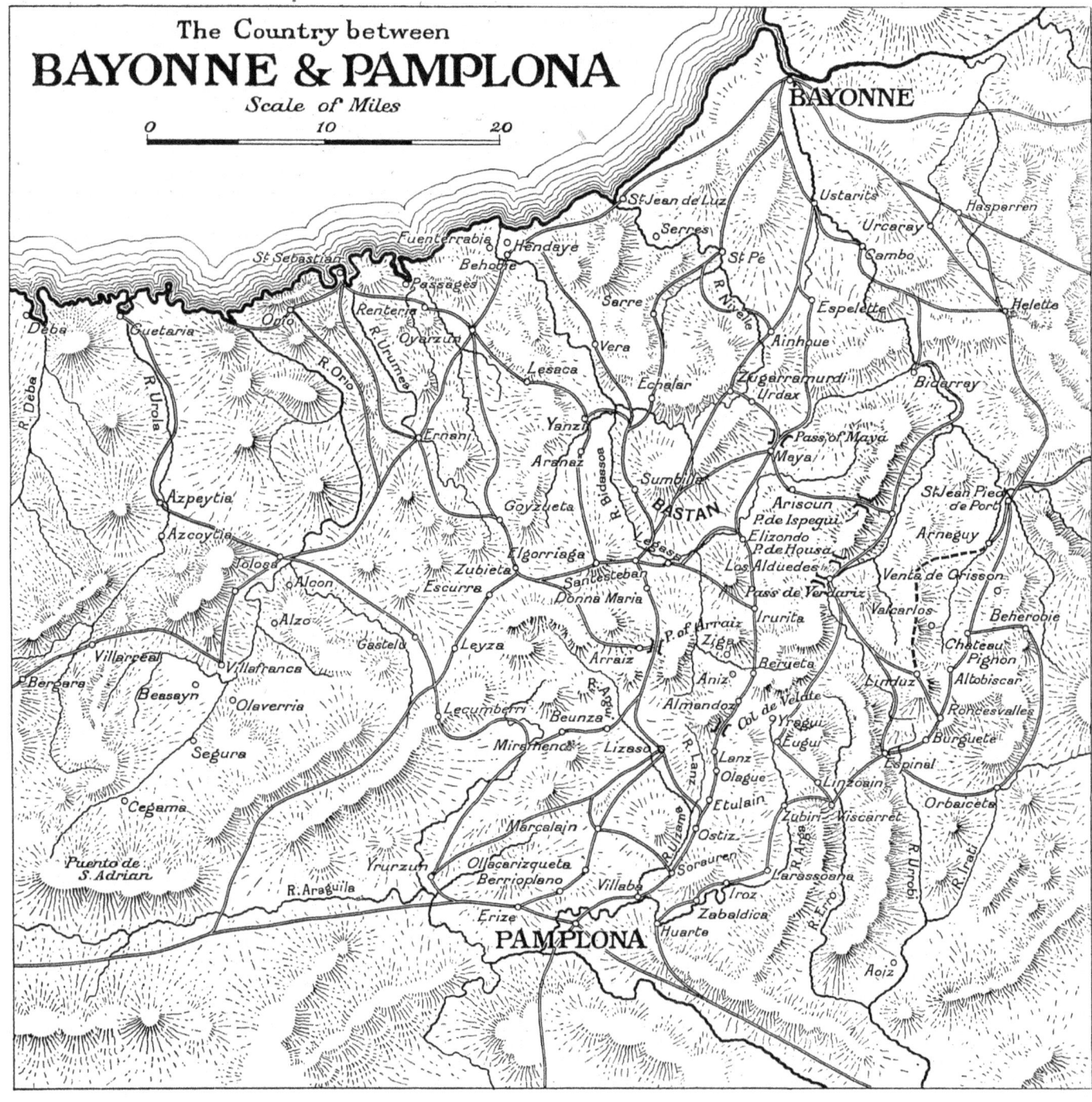

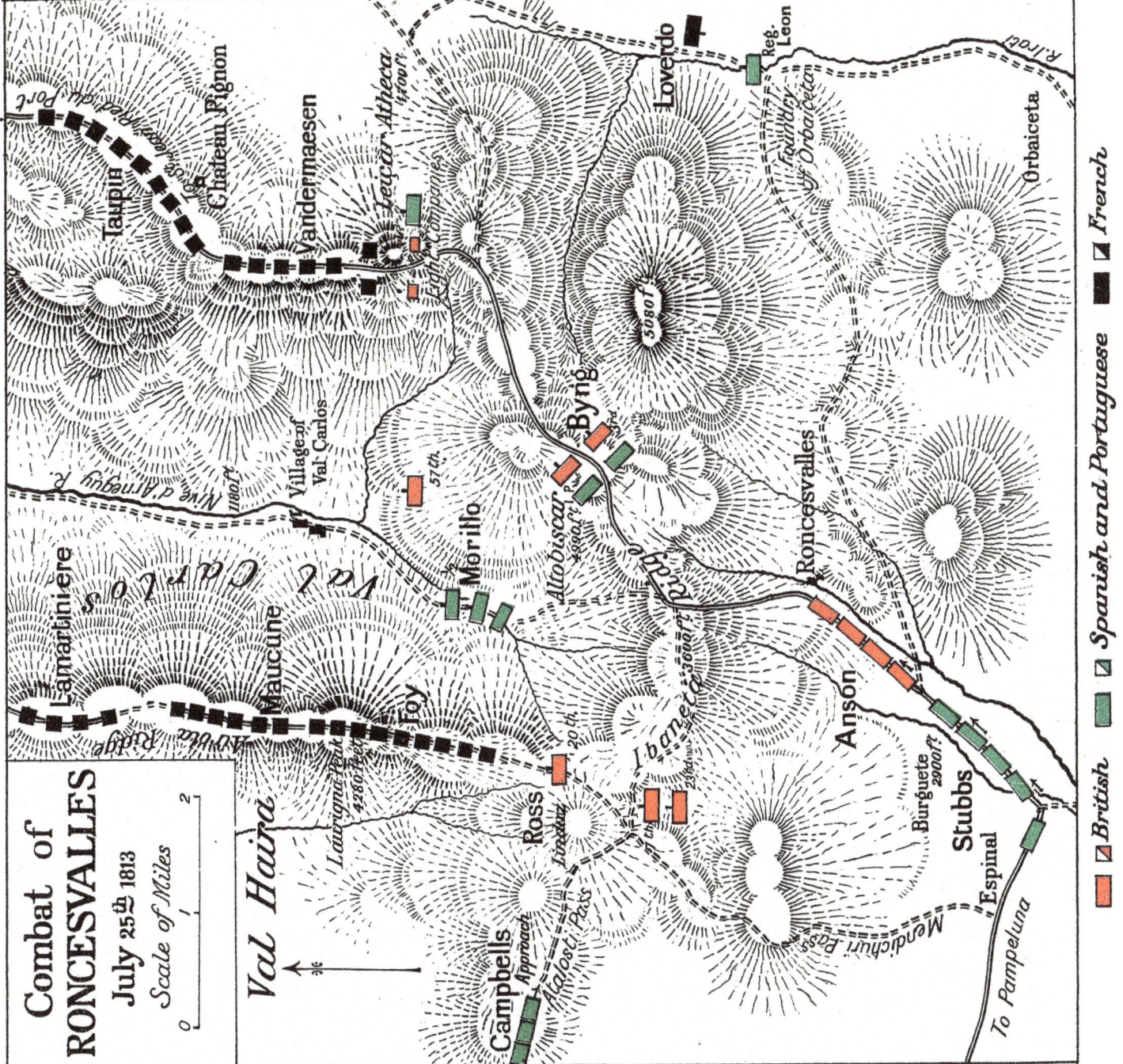

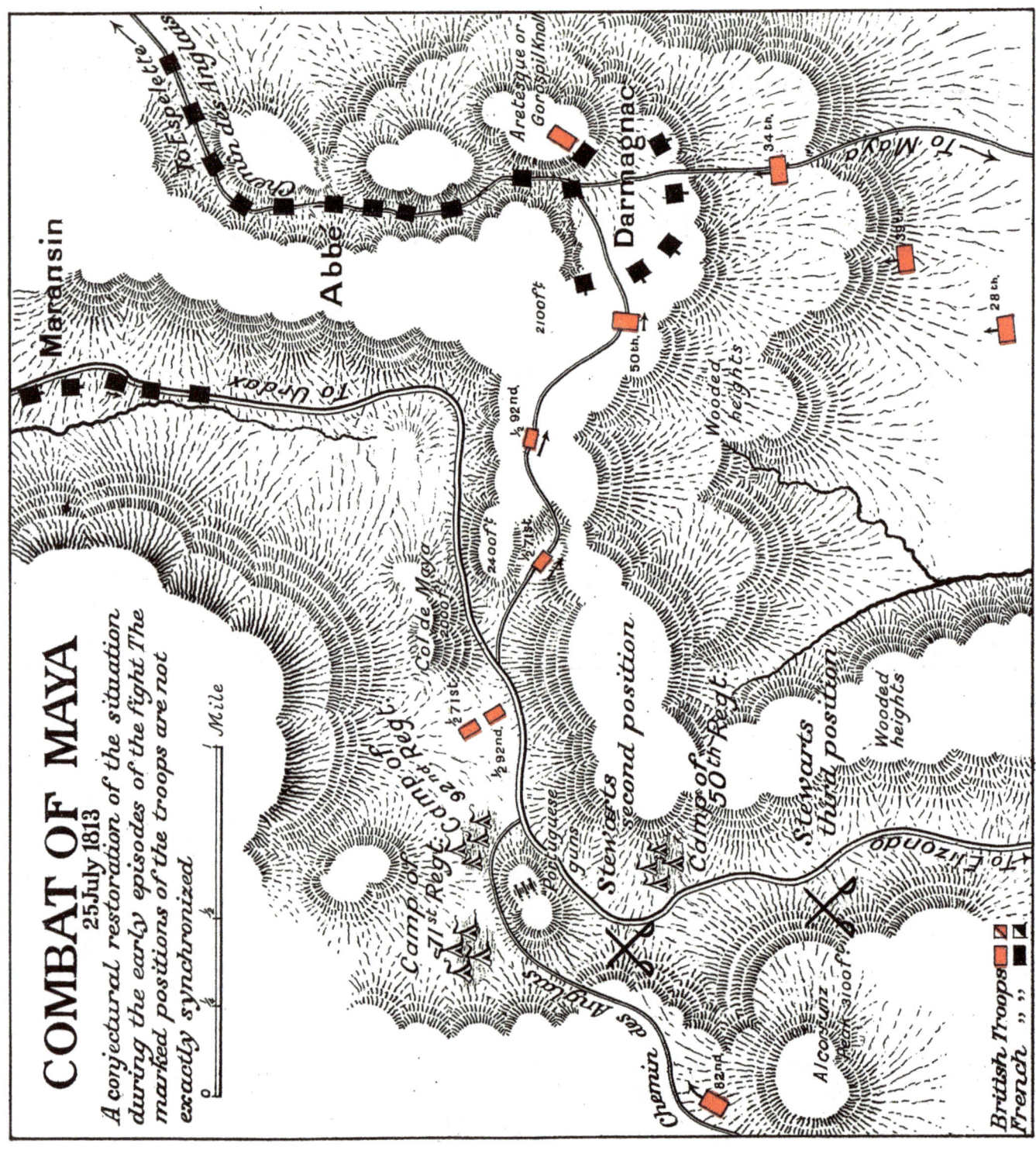

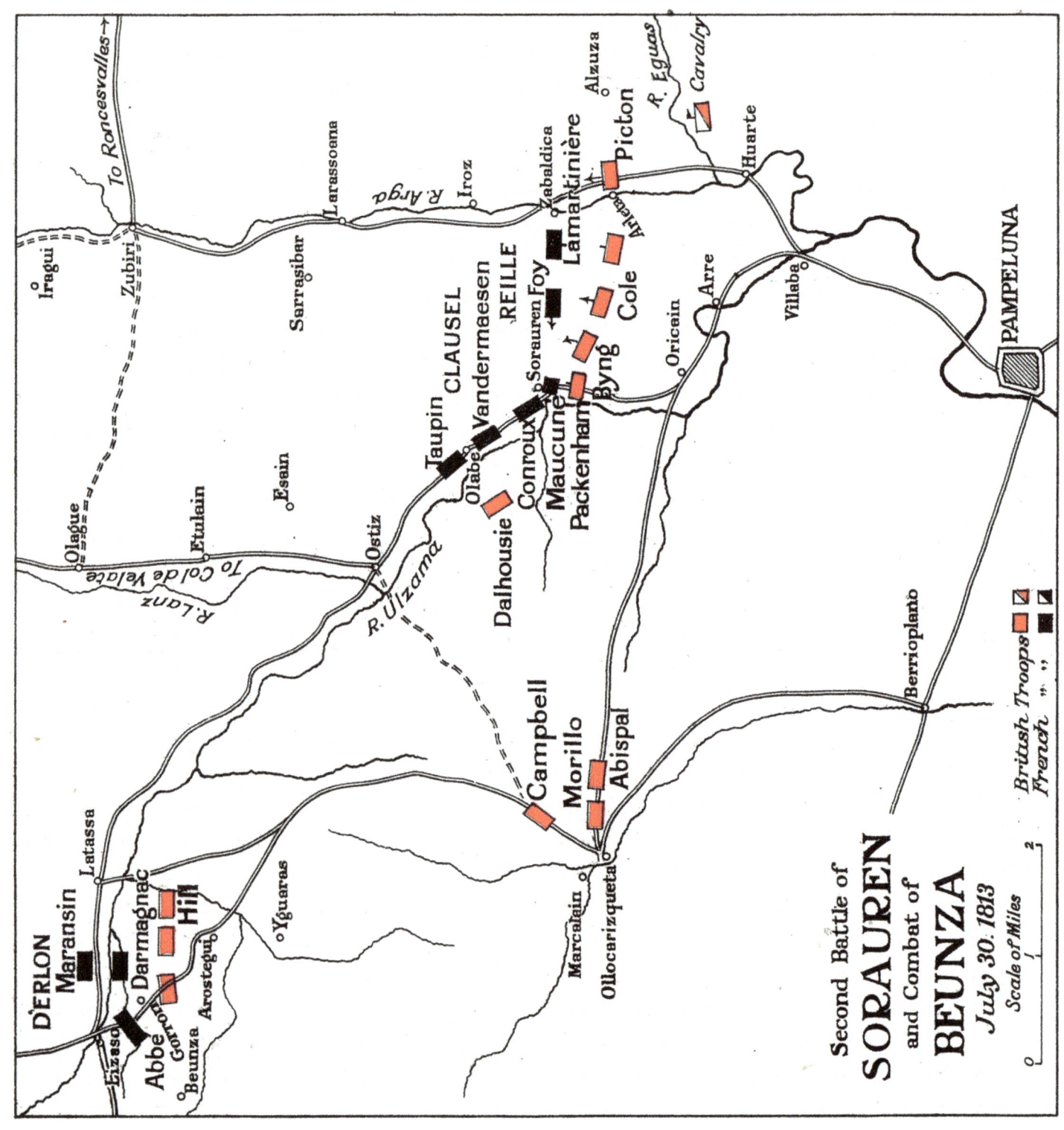

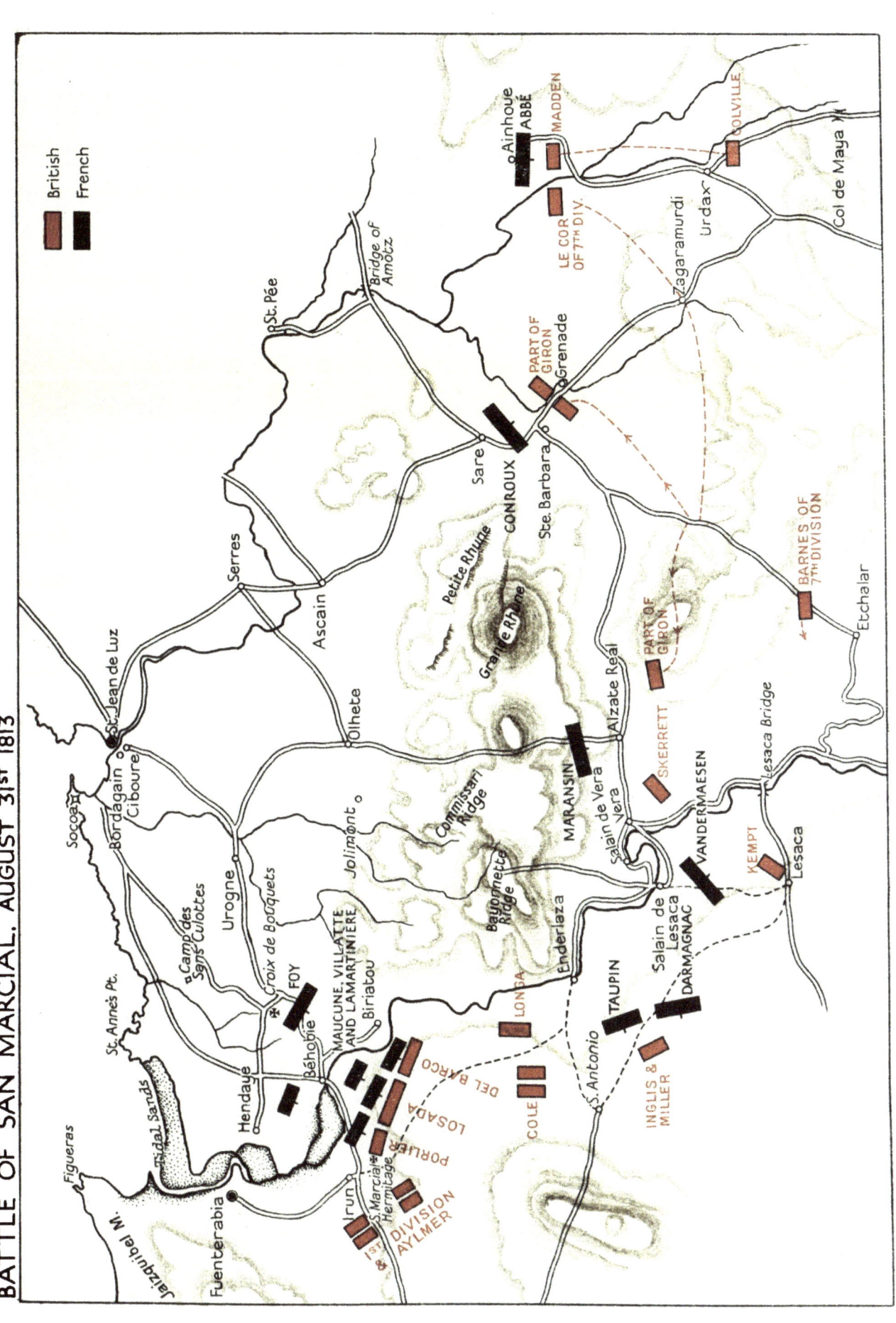

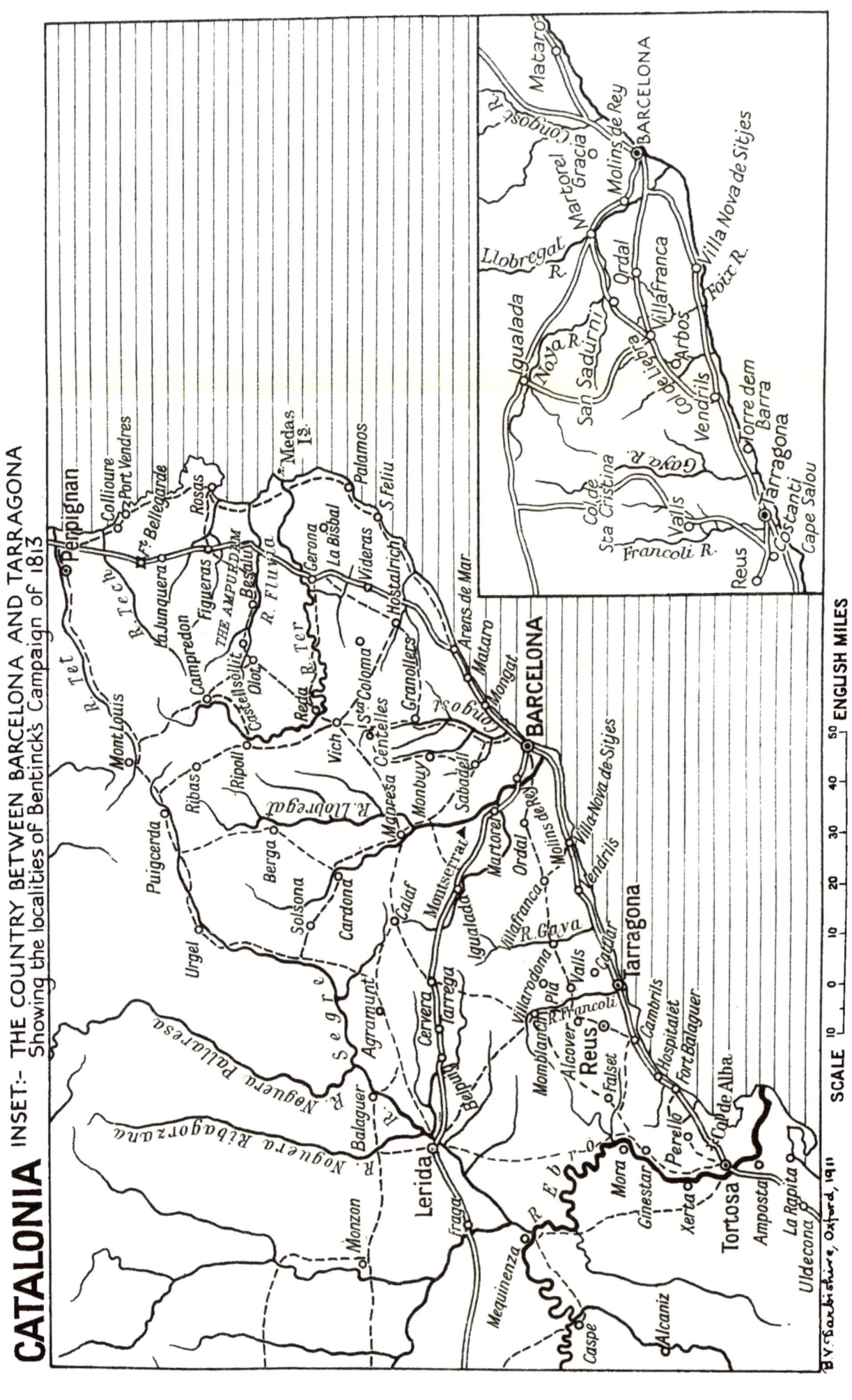

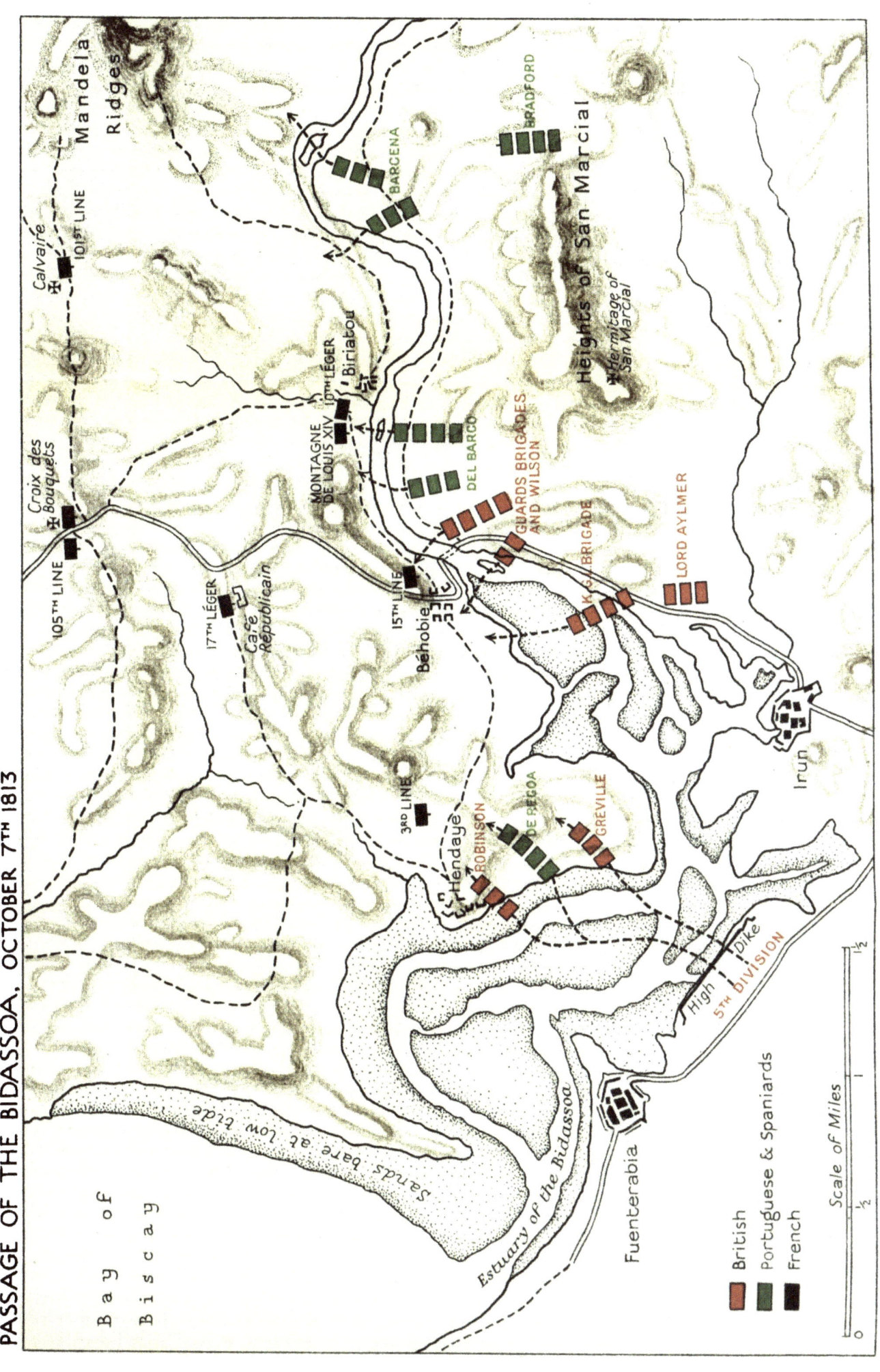

STORM OF THE FRENCH LINES ABOVE VERA, 17TH OCTOBER 1813

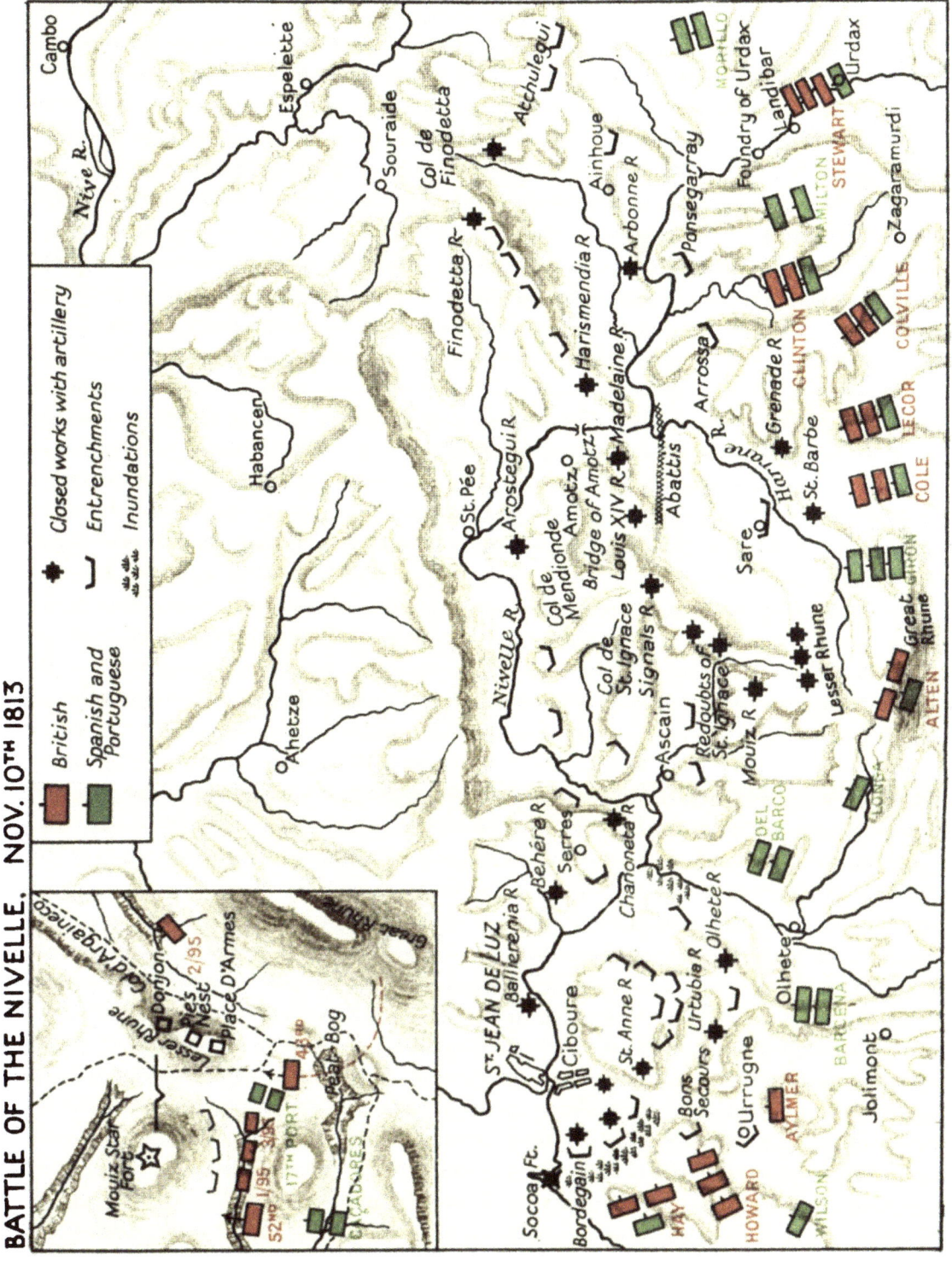

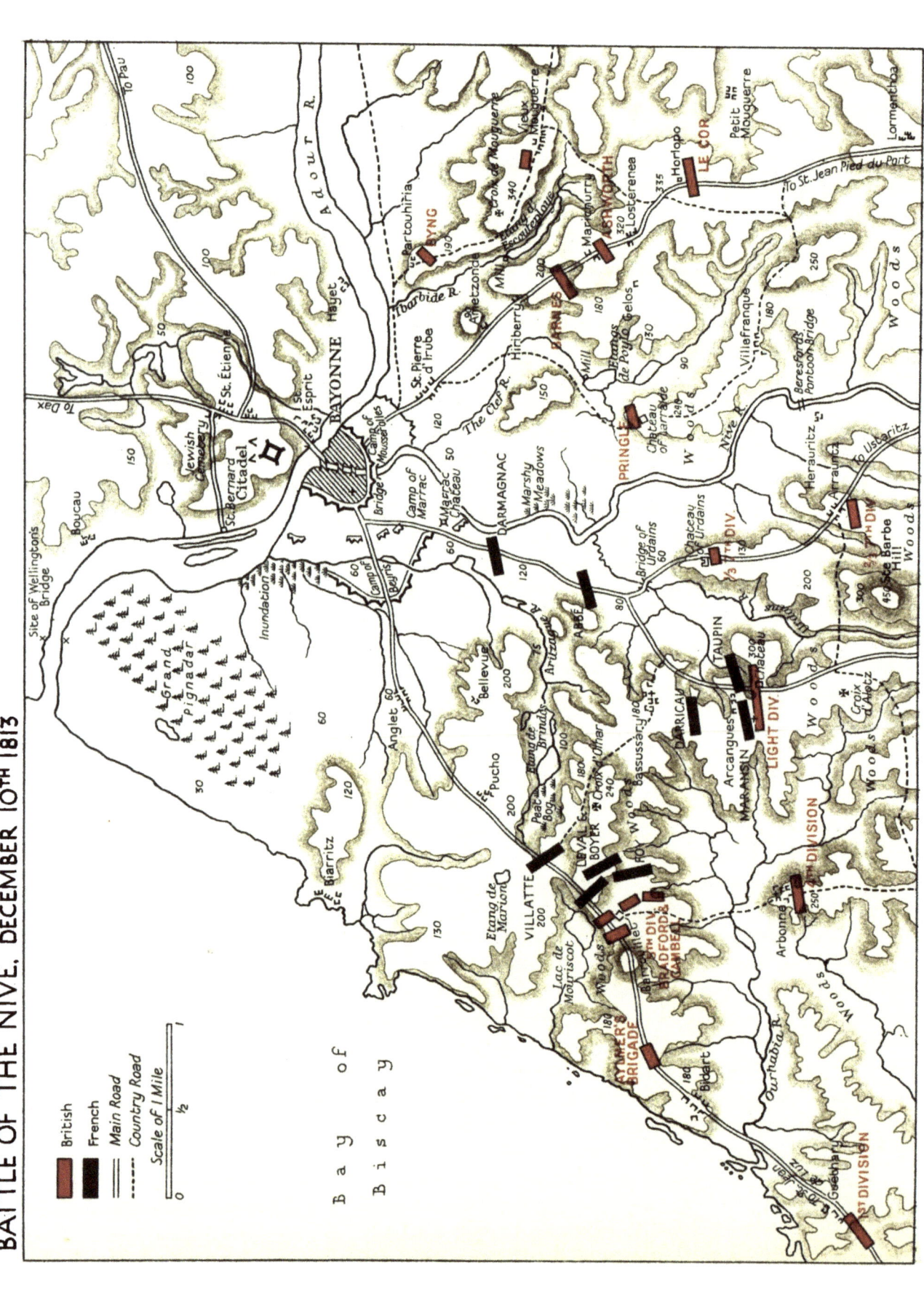

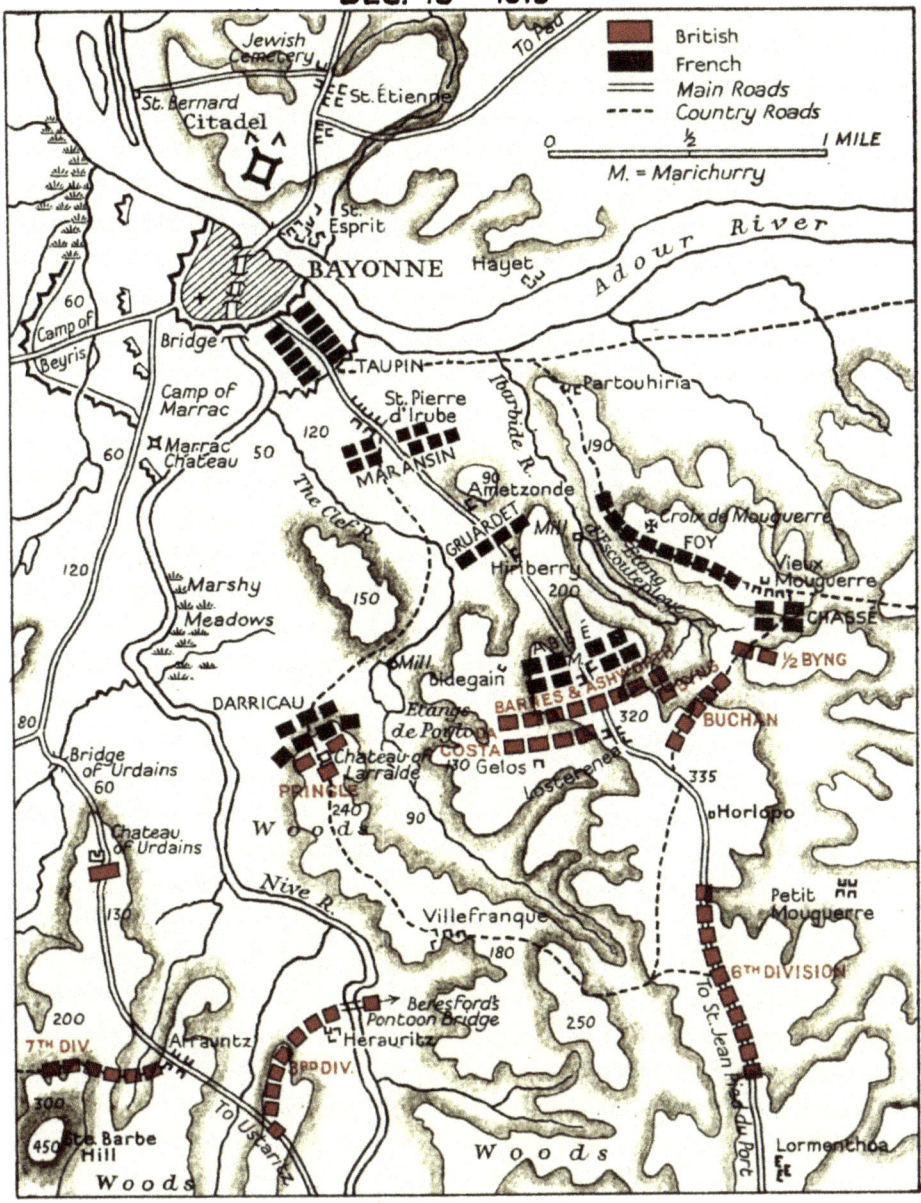

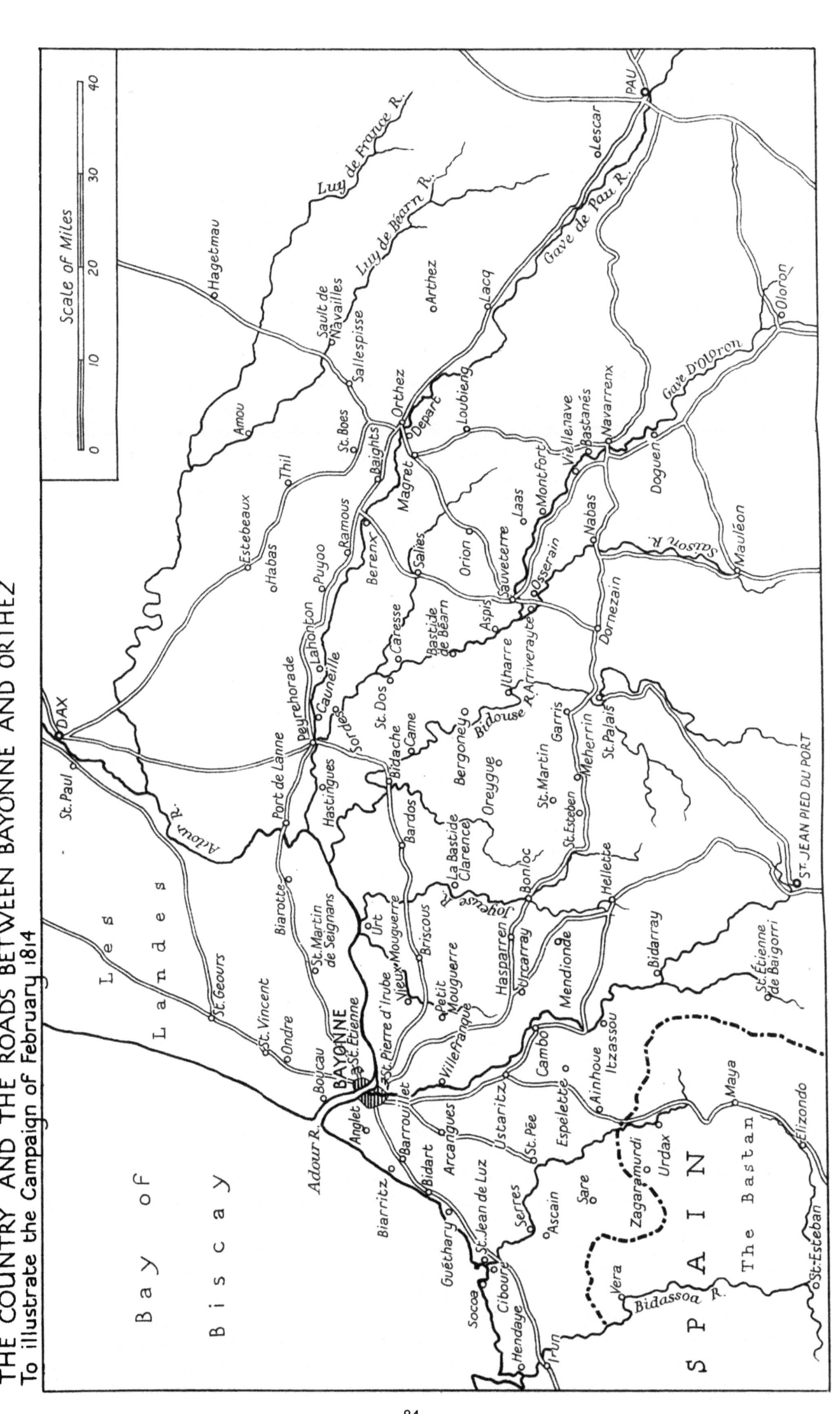

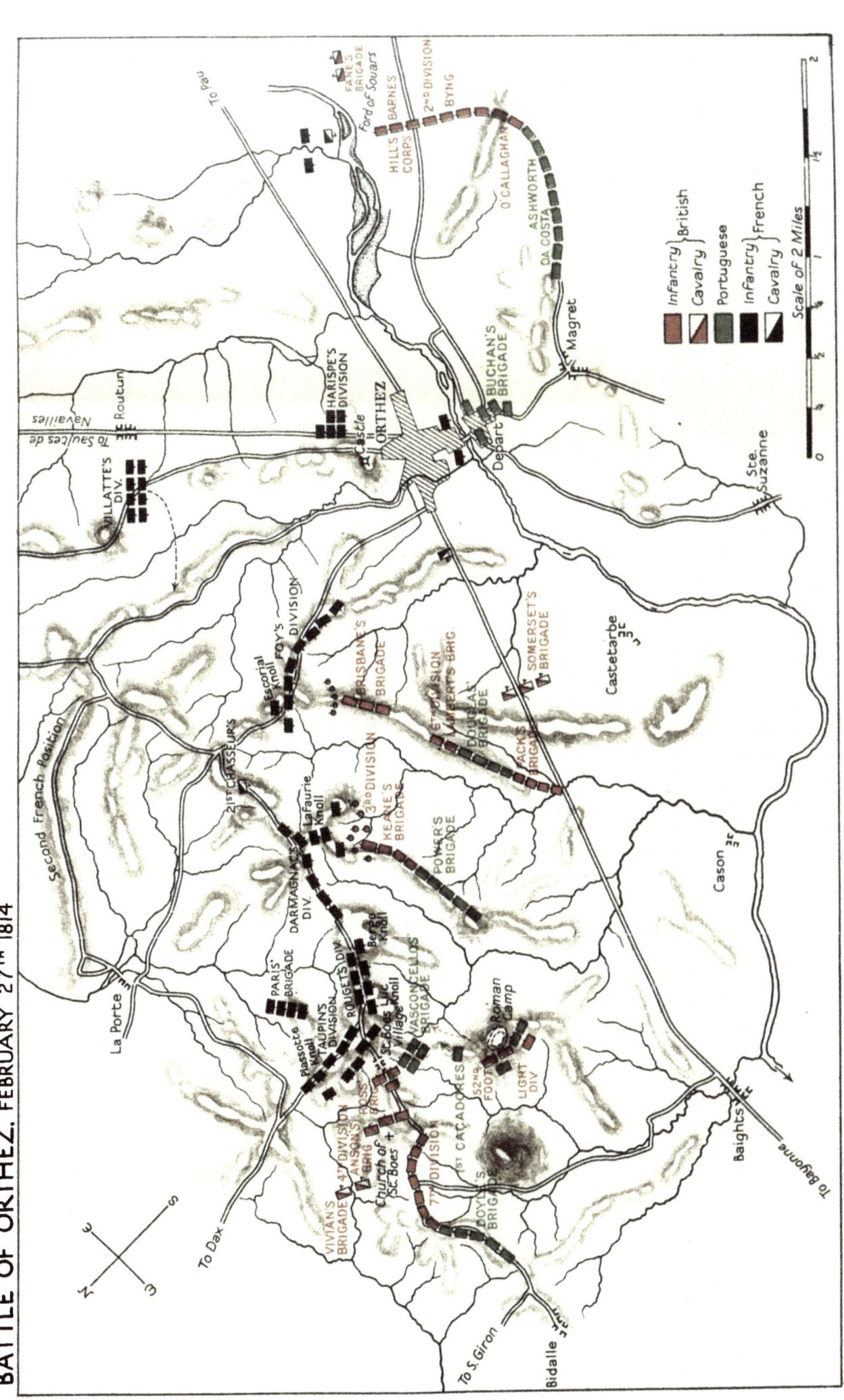

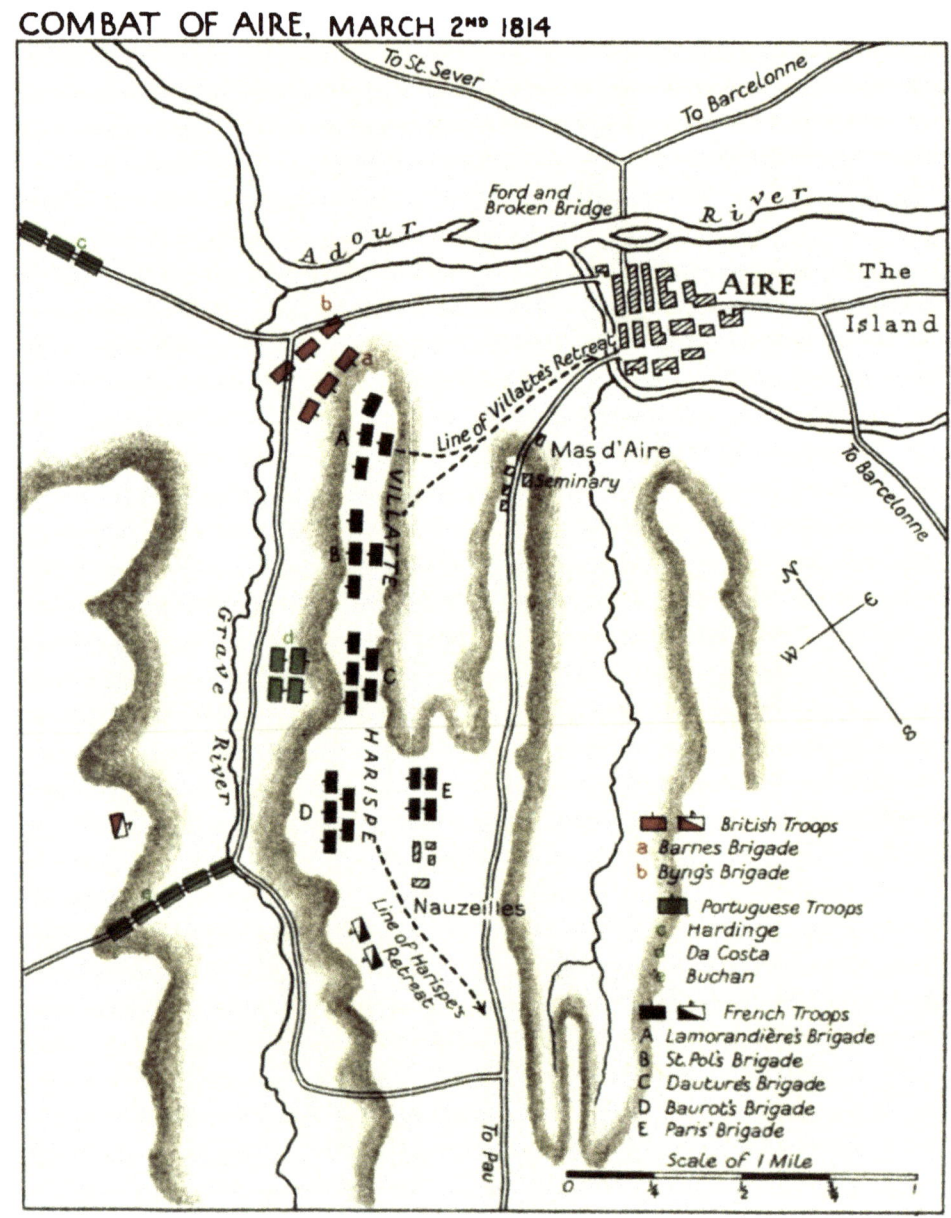

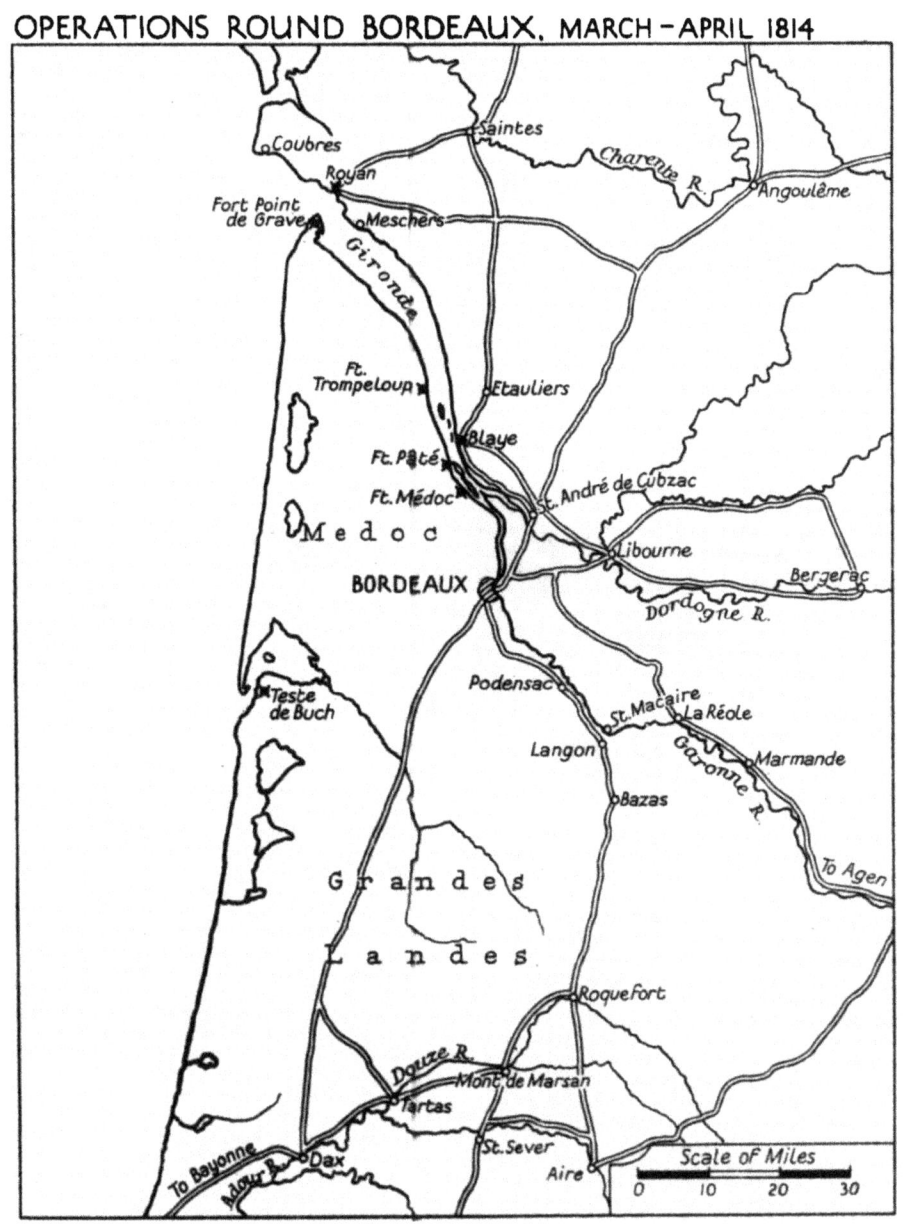

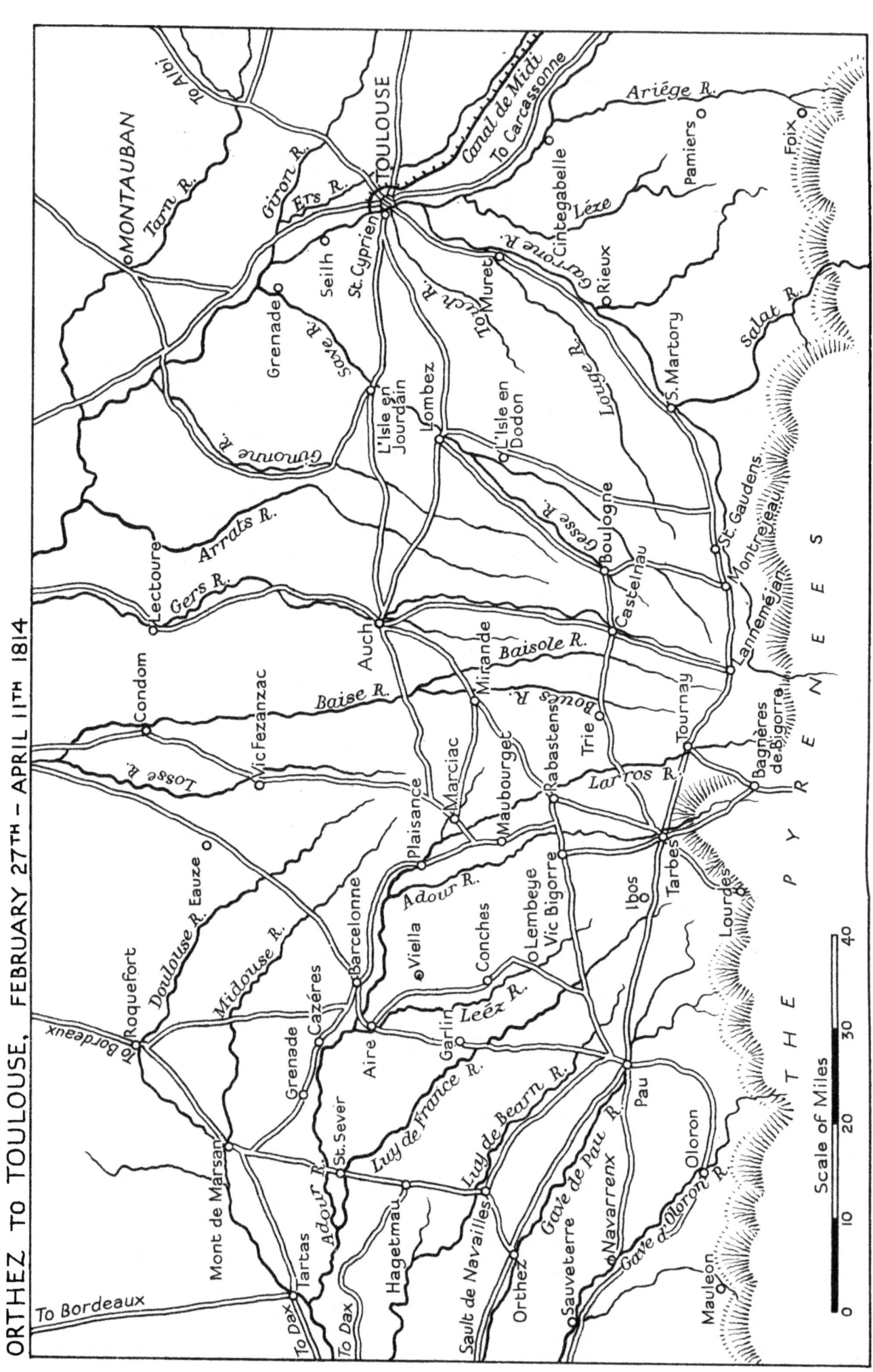

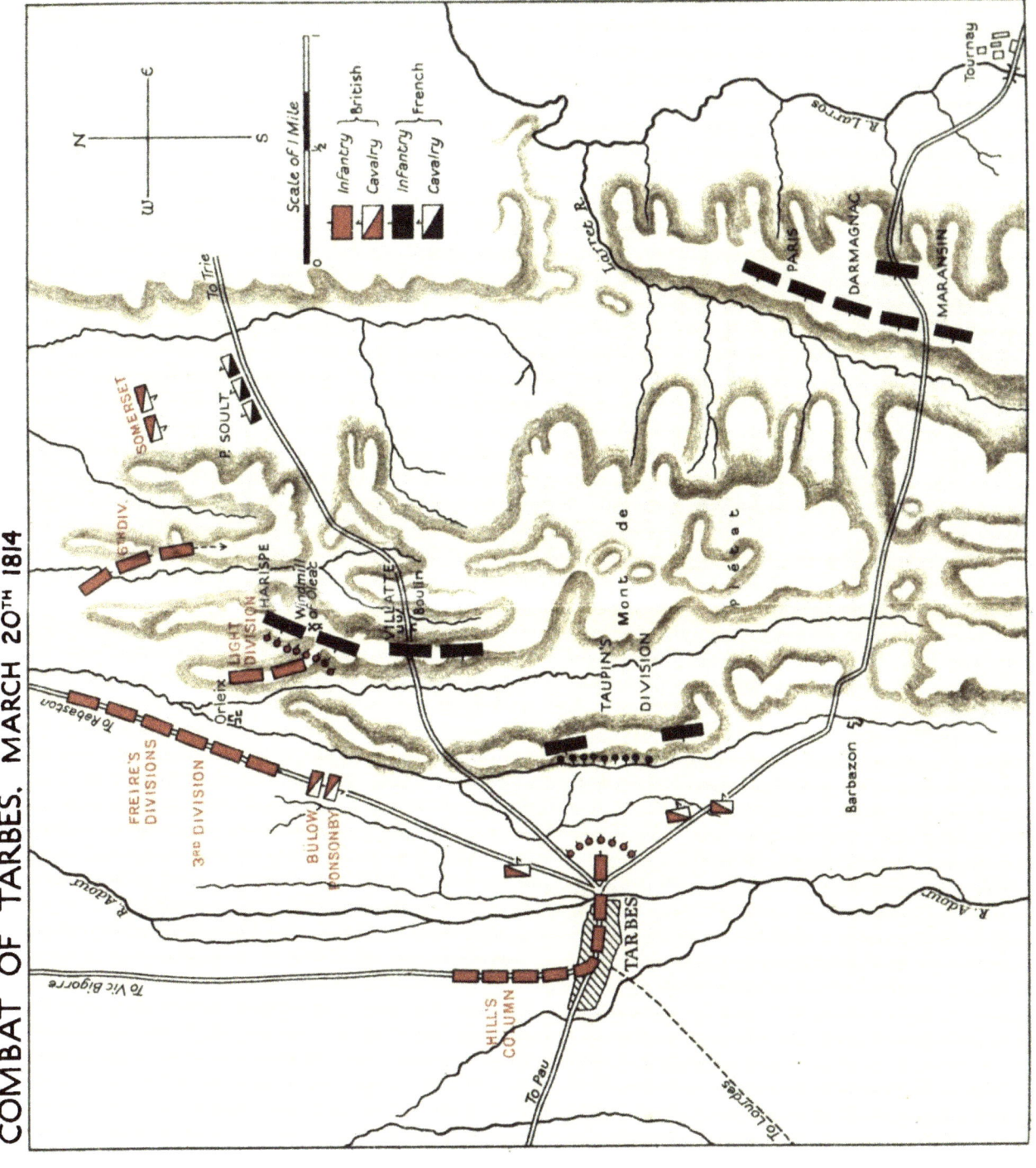

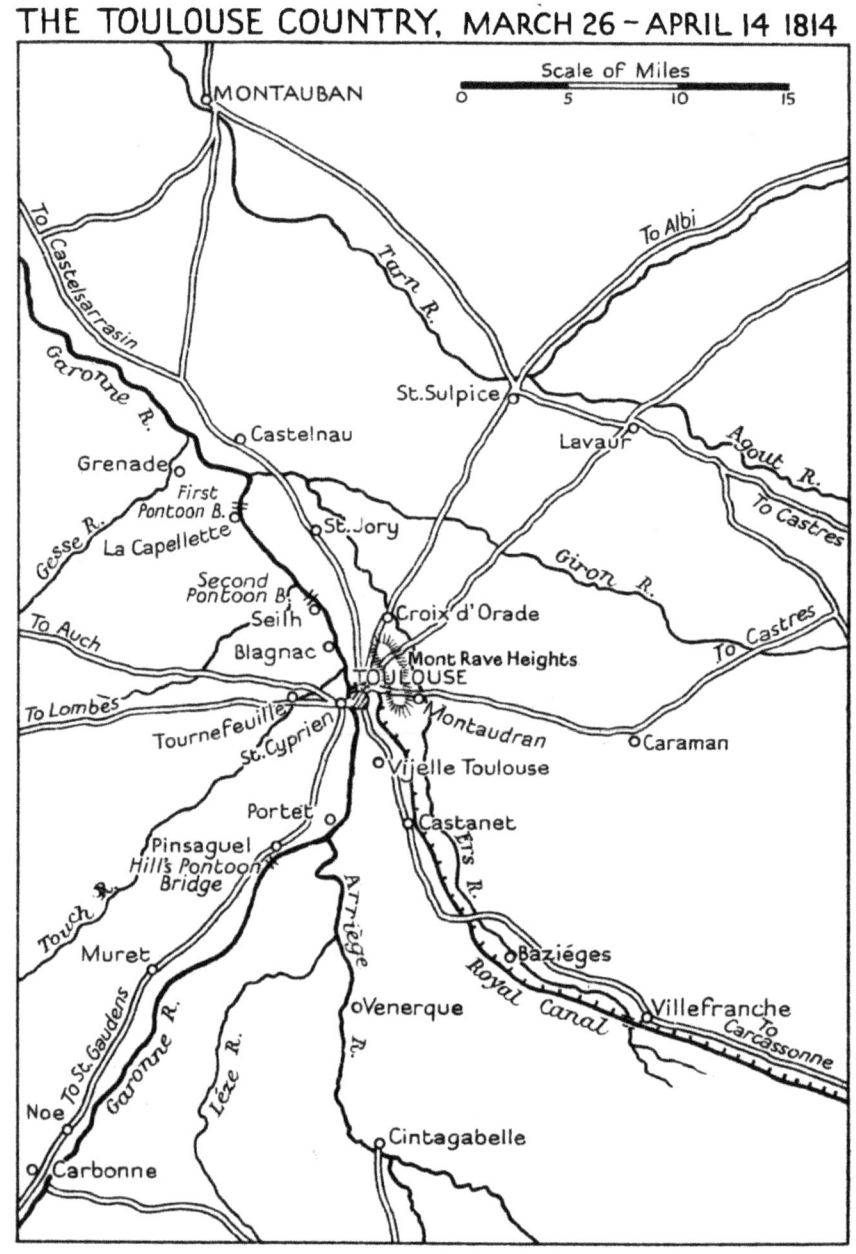

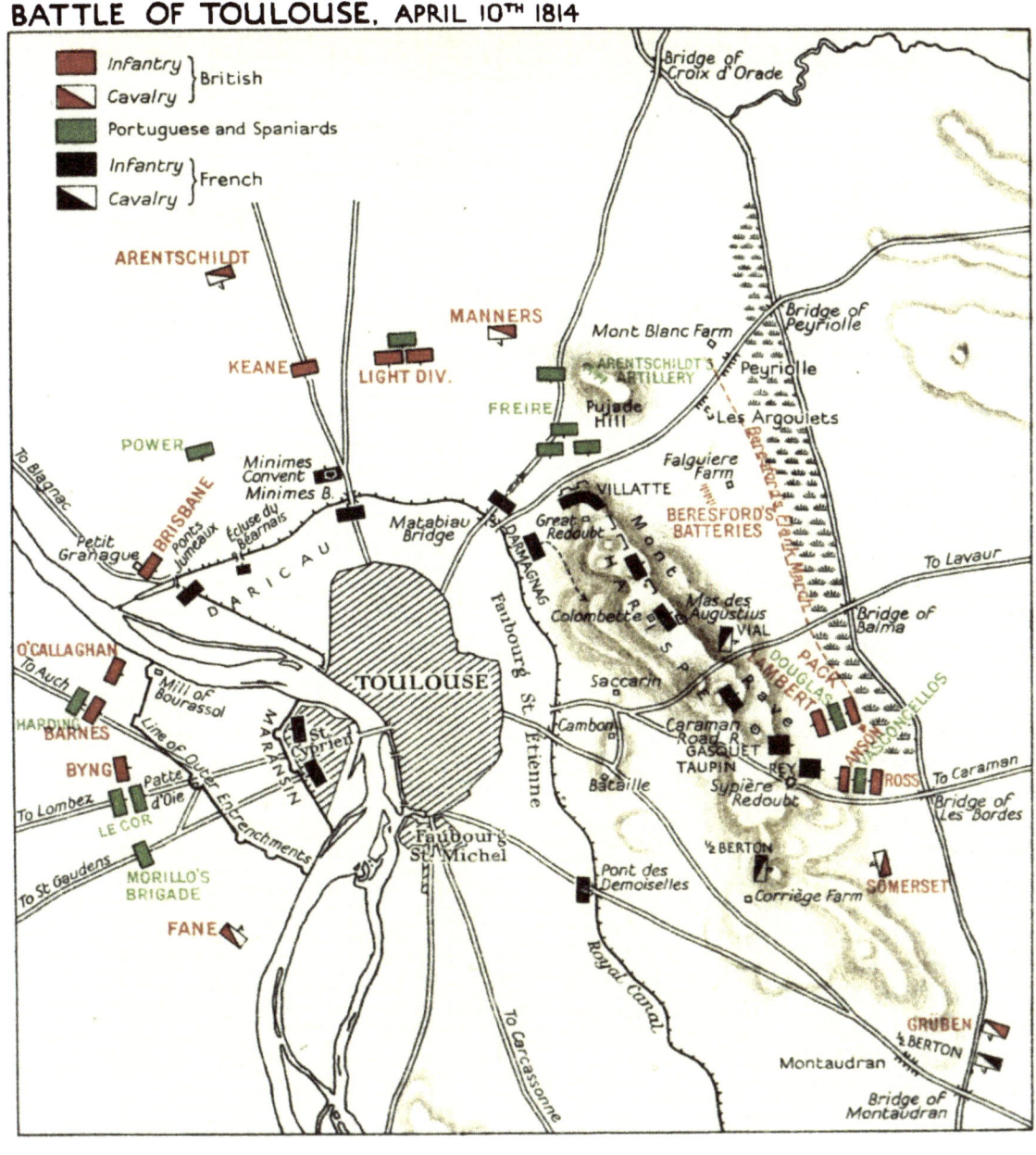

www.ingramcontent.com/pod-product-compliance
Lightning Source LLC
Chambersburg PA
CBHW040316240426
43664CB00028B/2940